Database design: a classified and annotated bibliography

THE BRITISH COMPUTER SOCIETY MONOGRAPHS IN
INFORMATICS

Editor: Professor P. A. Samet

Monographs in Informatics contain reports from BCS members and
specialist groups. The series publishes new research material and assesses
recent developments in a broad range of computer topics. Through the
Monographs in Informatics series computer scientists are able to share the
specialist knowledge of members of the Society, and at the same time
keep abreast of current research.

Some current titles:

Information Systems Methodologies
Eds. R. N. Maddison and G. J. Baker

Parallel Programming — A Bibliography
D. H. Bell, J. M. Kerridge, D. Simpson and N. Willis

User-orientated Command Language: Requirements and Designs
    for a Standard Job Control Language
Ed. K. Hopper

Computer Generated Output as Admissible Evidence in
    Civil and Criminal Cases
Eds. R. H. Sizer and A. Kelman

Microcomputer-Based Aids for the Disabled
Julia Schofield

Query Languages: A Unified Approach
Report of the Query Language Group

Buying Financial Accounting Software
BCS Auditing by Computer Specialist Group

Buying Payroll Software
BCS Auditing by Computer Specialist Group

Practical PL/I
G. R. Clarke, S. Green and P. Teague

Database Design: A Classified and Annotated Bibliography
M. Agosti

Database design: a classified and annotated bibliography

MARISTELLA AGOSTI
Facolta' di Scienze Statistiche
Universita' di Padova

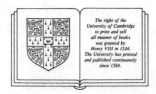

The right of the
University of Cambridge
to print and sell
all manner of books
was granted by
Henry VIII in 1534.
The University has printed
and published continuously
since 1584.

CAMBRIDGE UNIVERSITY PRESS
Cambridge
London   New York   New Rochelle
Melbourne   Sydney

Published by the Press Syndicate of the University of Cambridge
The Pitt Building, Trumpington Street, Cambridge CB2 1RP
32 East 57th Street, New York, NY 10022, USA
10 Oakleigh Road, Melbourne 3166, Australia

First published 1986

Printed in Great Britain at the
University Press, Cambridge

British Library cataloguing in publication data
  Agosti, Maristella
  Database design: a classified and annotated
  bibliography.–(The British Computer Society
  monographs in informatics)

  1. Database management–Bibliography   2. File
  organization (Computer Science)–Bibliography
  I. Title   II. Series
  016.00574   Z5643.D36

Library of Congress cataloguing data available

ISBN 0 521 31123 3

CONTENTS

FOREWORD

A rapidly growing area of application of information
technology is the use of databases. There is a large and
ever-increasing literature, there are proprietary packages
available by the hundred all making claims to solve the
world's problems. The non-specialist user is confused and is
not even sure what questions should be asked to decide on how
to establish a system that meets his needs. Dr Agosti's
carefully annotated bibliography of literature on the subject
up to the end of 1984 will be of considerable help to all,
specialist and non-specialist alike. It forms a welcome
addition to this series of monographs.

P.A. Samet
Editor,
British Computer Society,
Monographs in Informatics

PREFACE

1.0 INTRODUCTION

Database design is a process concerned with the construction of a database as a subsystem of an information system. Thus the database design process is an integral component of the information system design process. If the decision has been made to develop an application using database technology, the database design process can be started. Different related applications can be arranged to share the same database. The next section introduces the database design subject and the related terminology used to define a subject directory. In fact a list of subjects has been used as a directory to form a cross-reference to the pertinent documents. The references appear alphabetically later in the bibliography. Terms that have been defined by standard organisations or by other professional associations are adopted with the same meaning those bodies have ascribed to them; relevant references are (ISO, 1981), (ISO, 1982), and (SECT/IEEE, 1982).

Each reference includes the surname of the author(s) and the year of publication, for example, (Adiba, 1980) or (Adiba and Delobel, 1977). When the reference includes three or more authors, it reads (Adiba et al, 1976). The list of references is in alphabetical order by surname of the first author. In the case of multiple listings by a single author, the earliest publication appears first. When different references are given to an author alone or the author with others, all the single-author listings precede the multiple-author listings (e.g. (Chen, 1976), (Chen, 1982), (Chen et al, 1982)).

The abbreviations used are reported at the end of the preface. The abbreviations are not used in the reference title which is always reported as it is in the original text.

          The accents have been omitted from Italian and
French words.

     2.0 DISCUSSION

          The database design process is used to transform and
organise unstructured information and processing requirements
concerning the application, through different intermediate
representations, to a complex representation which defines
schemas and functional specifications. Various documents
which record the intermediate representations and the meanings
of all the pertinent classes of objects are produced during
this process. The database which is constructed during this
process is used in the enterprise for different purposes and
by diverse categories of users. Parts of the information
system which are supported by the computer are often referred
to as applications.

          The design process is usually divided into
components which produce intermediate representations. The
division into components is dependent upon the present
knowledge of the process and the present technology. The
divisions are useful for managing the process and permitting
the exchange of information and intermediate results between
the staff involved in the design. In the ensuing paragraphs
the underlined terms correspond with the headings in the
bibliography.

          The data stored in a database system is used
essentially to make decisions at the different levels of the
enterprise. The stored data concerns the information system
objects and their attributes; the meaning the users tend to
ascribe to the data can change in the different departments of
the enterprise and on the use they make of it. For these
reasons a major exercise has to be carried out in parallel
with the database design process. This is the construction of
a holder for the meanings ascribed by the designer to the data
held in the database. The data descriptions are called
metadata; the holder of them is called a data dictionary and
the system that manages it a data dictionary system.

          If it is shown in the preparatory cost/benefit
analysis of the application, that it is advisable to manage
the data with a database management system, then it will be
economical to make a substantial investment in the design of
the database, so that it can be used by diverse applications.
Errors made during the design process can affect the
application's entire life. The process therefore is of great
importance to the enterprise and it is necessary to pay much

attention to it.

The documents referring to the interface problems
with the information system area and other areas related to
the database design are grouped under the database design
'environment' heading. A subsequent section is devoted to the
system development processes (prototyping, ...); this section
refers to documents pertinent to this general topic.

The documents pertinent to information system design
methodologies are grouped under the heading information
systems design methodologies and evaluation.

So far a common consensus has not been reached on
the components the database design process must have. Most of
the authors agree on a division of the process into four or
five components (Lum et al, 1979), (Teorey and Fry, 1982) and
(Yao et al, 1982b); a division of the process into four
components is adopted in this bibliography:

1 Information requirements design;
2 Conceptual database design;
3 Implementation design;
4 Physical design.

The information requirements design is the first
component of the application design. It is the interface
between the analysis process and the design process. It
represents the process of mapping analysis into design. It
leads to the specification of the design requirements for the
pertinent part of the information system to meet the
information requirements of the enterprise.

The conceptual database design component leads to
the construction of the conceptual schema which provides a
unique central description of the various information contents
that may be in the database. The conceptual schema is a
DBMS-independent information structure which is obtained
through the consolidation of the user information requirements
specifications. Both the static (or passive) and the dynamic
(or active) characteristics of the data are taken into
consideration.

The implementation design incorporates the
conceptual model into the structure of the selected database
management system and analyses the possible transactions. The
file design starts in this component together with the access
paths study.

The physical design component serves to construct the storage schema. The physical space for records and indices and the physical media that are to be utilised are defined.

The logical database design term has not been used to name one design component, because it has so many different meanings in the literature and its use can only cause confusion. Also conceptual design can be a misleading term because it is applied to different practices; the conceptual design component is meant to embrace the integration of all the concepts which are necessary to support the various application views of data; the conceptual design produces a conceptual view of data in which the particularities of specific views of data are resolved (Smith et al, 1982). The documents that deal with the conceptual design at a very general level are grouped under conceptual modelling.

The meaning ascribed to data design is that introduced by Wasserman and Botnick in (Wasserman and Botnick, 1981). That is a wide range of topics on data structures and database design. In particular the topics across the programming languages/database management interface and the design techniques that propose systematic methods for the design activity.

Data analysis refers to the techniques which study the nature of the data pertinent to the application.

Different categories of users have different targets in their work and they tend to see the data from different perspectives or views; a view is the representation of a portion of the application and it is the part that a group of users needs to deal with most often for data management. A snapshot of a selected portion of the database allows some applications to view the database 'as of' a specific time without having to execute a query at that specific time (Adiba and Lindsay, 1980). The problem of mapping is referred to in the appropriate section.

A data model is a way of representing data and its interrelationships. A data model describes the data of the pertinent part of the information system, because it can be used as a tool for capturing the meaning of data as related to the complete meaning of the information system. Diverse data models are usually used in the different components of the database design process to describe the data of the pertinent part of the application. In the conceptual database design component a semantic data model is adopted, where semantic data model identifies all the data models that have been constructed to explicity capture the semantics of the data

with their constructs. The semantic data model derives its
name from the fact that it is used during the conceptual
design to capture the meaning, or semantics, of the
application. While a processable data model is used in the
implementation design component. It is called processable
because the data representations, or schema, are processable
by the computer. Thus the data models play a major role in
the database design process and a section has been devoted to
the subject.

The database design methodologies, techniques, and
methods which are practiced today are part of the development
techniques for computer-based systems. Their development is
directly effected by the developments taking place in related
areas such as programming languages and hardware technology.
A "database design methodology" is an integrated collection of
methods and techniques, which supports the complete database
design process. A "technique" in this design context provides
a systematic way of doing a part of the design. When a
technique is applied correctly, it leads to a foreseeable
result. A technique does not fulfil the requirements of
integration and completeness that are required of a
methodology. A "method" is an organised set of ideas that are
used in doing a specific activity. It is a formal way of
doing the design of only an activity. Several database design
methods, techniques and methodologies have been developed and
proposed in literature; the database design methodologies,
methods and techniques section indexes pertinent documents.
The design of new database architecures section addresses new
design approaches.

The distributed database design section refers to
papers which are focused on the distribution of the
application.

The section on reference models for the database
design process refers to papers which are concerned with the
construction or the use of a general framework of the database
design process.

The database design process is complex and many
different aspects need to be addressed by the designer. The
keeping of the design documentation consistent with the design
development and modification requires a big effort. The
database restructuring, reorganisation and conversion section
indexes documents on the different aspects of modification of
a database. Computer aided database design tools are being
developed to support the designer in one or more components of
the design process; pertinent papers are referred to in the
computer aided database design section.

Relevant standards and ANSI/X3/SPARC, the last two terms of the directory, refer to relevant activities of bodies concerned with international standards.

ACKNOWLEDGEMENTS

The research necessary for the preparation of this bibliography would not been possible without the effective help of the librarians of the Main Library of the Thames Polytechnic, London, to whom sincere thanks are due.

ABBREVIATIONS AND ACRONYMS

ACM	Assoc. for Computing Machinery
AICA	Assoc. It. di Informatica e di Calcolo Automatico
Ann.	Annual
Archit.	Architecture
Assoc.	Association, Associazione
BCS	British Computer Society
Bull.	Bulletin
CADD	Computer Aided Database Design
Chap.	Chapter
Co.	Company
Comm.	Communications
Conf.	Conference
CREST	EEC Scientific and Technical Research Committee
DB	Database(s)
DBMS	DB Management System(s)
DBS	Database System
DDB	Distributed Database(s)
DDBMS	Distributed DBMS(s)
DD/D	Data Dictionary/Directory systems
DDL	Data Definition Language
DDS	Data Dictionary System
DDSWP	Data Dictionary Systems Working Party
DML	Data Manipulation Language
Dept.	Department
Doc.	Document
Ed(s)	Editor(s), Edition
Engin.	Engineering, Engineer(s)
E/R	Entity-Relationship
IEEE	The Institute of Electrical and Electronics Engin.
IFIP	International Federation for Information Processing
Inform.	Information
Int.	International
IS	Information System(s)
ISO	Int. Organization for Standardization
It.	Italiano, Italiana, Italian
Jour.	Journal
Lab.	Laboratory
Ltd.	Limited
MIS	Management Information Systems
Nat.	National

NBS	United States (US) National Bureau of Standards
No.	Number
NYU	New York University
OSI	Open Systems Interconnection
p(p).	page(s)
Prin.	Principles
Proc.	Proceedings
Pub.	Publication(s), Publisher or Publishing
RDBMS	Relational DBMS
Rep.	Report
Res.	Research
Ser.	Series
SIGMOD	Special Interest Group on Management of Data
Surv.	Survey(s)
Symp.	Symposium
Syst.	System(s)
TC	Technical Committee
Tech.	Technical, Technology
Trans.	Transactions
Univ.	University
VLDB	Very Large Data Bases
Vol.	Volume
WG	Working Group

Short form of each month name.

The abbreviation of each state of the USA used with zip code.

LIST OF SUBJECTS

GENERAL

Database design 'environment'
System development processes (prototyping, ...)
Conceptual modelling
Data design
Data models
Data analysis

COMPONENTS OF THE DATABASE DESIGN PROCESS

Information requirements design
Conceptual database design
Implementation design
Physical design
Design versions

OTHER ASPECTS OF THE DESIGN

Mapping
Snapshots
Views

DATA DICTIONARY SYSTEMS

Data dictionary systems

METHODOLOGIES AND REFERENCE MODELS

Information systems design methodologies and evolution
Database design methodologies, methods and techniques

Reference models for the database design process
Design of new database architectures

MANAGEMENT OF THE DESIGN

Computer aided database design
Database restructuring, reorganisation and conversion

DISTRIBUTED DESIGN

Distributed database design

STANDARDS

Relevant standards
ANSI/X3/SPARC

GENERAL

Database design 'environment'

(Amble et al, 1979)
(Atre, 1980)
(Baker and Holloway, 1984)
(Bhabuta, 1984)
(Bubenko et al, 1978)
(Ceri, 1980)
(Champine et al, 1980)
(Chen and Yao, 1977)
(Cookson, 1983)
(Couger et al, 1982)
(Date, 1981a)
(DDBWG/BCS, 1983)
(Deen and Hammersley, 1980)
(Fry and Teorey, 1978)
(GAO, 1979)
(Hainaut, 1981)
(Inmon, 1981)
(Kambayashi et al, 1982)
(Kent, 1981b)
(McCracken and Jackson, 1982)
(Maggiolini, 1981)
(Mumford, 1984)
(Nijssen, 1976b)
(Olle et al, 1982)
(Stamper, 1977)
(Sundgren, 1975)
(Sundgren, 1978)
(Teorey et al, 1982)
(Ullman, 1980)
(Wasserman et al, 1981)
(Weber and Wasserman, 1979)
(Wiederhold, 1977)
(Wood-Harper and Fitzgerald, 1982)
(Yao et al, 1982a)
(Yao and Kunii, 1982)

System development processes (prototyping, ...)

(Alavi, 1984a)
(Alavi, 1984b)
(BCS/ISADWP, 1984)
(Boehm et al, 1984)
(Champine et al, 1980)
(Couger et al, 1982)
(McCraken and Jackson, 1982)
(Nijssen, 1978)

Conceptual modelling

(Biller and Neuhold, 1976)
(Brodie, 1980)
(Brodie and Zilles, 1980)
(Bubenko, 1977a)
(Falkenberg, 1976)
(Gallaire et al, 1984)
(Hoare, 1972)
(ISO, 1981)
(ISO, 1982)
(Jajodia et al, 1983)
(Lindencrona-Ohlin, 1979)
(Moulin et al, 1976)
(Nijssen, 1976a)
(Nijssen, 1977a)
(Rolland, 1983)
(Schmid, 1977)
(Smith and Smith, 1977a)
(Smith and Smith, 1977b)
(Smith and Smith, 1982)

Data design

(Brodie, 1980)
(Brodie, 1981)
(Hoare, 1972)
(Kent, 1977)
(Kent, 1978)
(Kent, 1981a)
(Kerschberg et al, 1980)
(Leavenworth, 1981)
(Lum et al, 1984)
(Moulin et al, 1976)
(Rothnie and Hardgrave, 1976)
(Smith and Smith, 1977a)
(Smith and Smith, 1977b)
(Wasserman and Botnick, 1981)

(Weber, 1976)
(Weller and York, 1984)

Data models

(Abrial, 1974)
(Bachman and Daya, 1977)
(Borkin, 1980)
(Bowers, 1984)
(Bracchi et al, 1976)
(Brodie, 1982)
(Brodie and Schmidt, 1981)
(Brown and Parker, 1983)
(Chan, 1982)
(Chen, 1976)
(Chen, 1982)
(Codd, 1970)
(Codd, 1979)
(Colombetti et al, 1978)
(Date, 1981a)
(Data, 1981b)
(Davenport, 1979b)
(Deen, 1980)
(Delobel, 1980)
(Dos Santos et al, 1979)
(El-Masri and Wiederhold, 1979)
(Falkenberg, 1976)
(Hall et al, 1976)
(Hawryszkiewycz, 1980)
(Kent, 1976)
(Kerschberg et al, 1976)
(Matsuka et al, 1982)
(Ong et al, 1984)
(Parent, 1981)
(Parimala et al, 1984)
(Rothnie and Hardgrave, 1976)
(Sakai, 1979)
(Schiel, 1982)
(Shipman, 1981)
(Solvberg, 1979)
(Stoker et al, 1984)
(Tsichritzis and Lochovsky, 1982)
(Tsur and Zaniolo, 1984)
(Weber, 1976)
(Wong and Mylopoulos, 1977)
(Yao et al, 1982c)

Data analysis

(Baker, 1982)
(Cookson, 1983)
(Davenport, 1978)
(Davenport, 1979b)
(Hackett, 1981)
(Palmer, 1978)
(Shave, 1981)
(Symons and Tijsma, 1982)
(Wood-Harper and Fitzgerald, 1982)

COMPONENTS OF THE DATABASE DESIGN PROCESS

Information requirements design

(Bracchi et al, 1979)
(Bubenko, 1981)
(Davis, 1981)
(Demo and Marini, 1980)
(Heitmeyer and McLean, 1983)
(Kahn, 1976)
(Lum et al, 1979)
(Shu et al, 1980)
(Taggart and Tharp, 1977)
(Teorey and Fry, 1980)
(Yadav, 1983)
(Yao et al, 1982c)

Conceptual database design

(Batini et al, 1980)
(Benci et al, 1976)
(Biller and Neuhold, 1977)
(Breutmann et al, 1979)
(Brodie and Silva, 1982)
(Brown and Parker, 1983)
(Bubenko, 1977b)
(Bubenko, 1979)
(Ceri et al, 1981a)
(Codd, 1979)
(Curtice and Jones, 1982)
(Davenport, 1979a)
(De et al, 1981)
(De Antonellis and Zonta, 1981)
(El-Masri and Wiederhold, 1979)
(Falkenberg, 1980)

(Frost, 1983)
(Fry and Teorey, 1978)
(Gross et al, 1980)
(Hawryszkiewycz, 1980)
(Housel et al, 1979)
(ISO, 1981)
(ISO, 1982)
(Jajodia et al, 1983)
(Lum et al, 1979)
(Machgeels, 1976)
(Meltzer, 1976)
(Mijares et al, 1976)
(Navathe and Gadgil, 1982)
(Navathe and Schkolnick, 1978)
(Nijssen, 1977b)
(Nijssen, 1978)
(Oftedal and Solvberg, 1981)
(Olle, 1978)
(Oren and Aschim, 1979)
(Parent, 1981)
(Raver and Hubbard, 1977)
(Ruchti, 1976)
(Sakai, 1981)
(Solvberg, 1979)
(Teorey and Fry, 1980)
(Yormark, 1977)
(Zaniolo and Melkanoff, 1982)

Implementation design

(Fry and Teorey, 1978)
(Irani et al, 1979)
(Lum et al, 1979)
(Prakash et al, 1984)
(Prowse and Johnson, 1980)
(Philips and Jackson, 1984)
(Rolin, 1980)
(Wilmot, 1984)

Physical design

(Bell, 1984)
(Bell and Deen, 1984)
(Bonfatti et al, 1983)
(Carlis et al, 1983)
(Christodoulakis, 1984)
(Davis and Coumpas, 1984)
(Finkelstein et al, 1982)
(Fry and Teorey, 1978)

(Gross et al, 1980)
(Jarke and Koch, 1984)
(Lum et al, 1979)
(March, 1983)
(March and Severance, 1978)
(Philips and Jackson, 1984)
(Reuter and Kinzinger, 1984)
(Sarda and Isaac, 1981)
(Schkolnick, 1978)
(Schkolnick, 1982)
(Severance and Carlis, 1977)
(Stocker, 1977)
(Teorey and Fry, 1980)
(Whang et al, 1981)

Design versions

(Katz and Lehman, 1984)

OTHER ASPECTS OF THE DESIGN

Mapping

(Kalinichenko, 1976)
(Keller and Ullman, 1984)
(Paolini and Pelagatti, 1977)

Snapshots

(Adiba, 1980)
(Adiba and Lindsay, 1980)

Views

(Adiba, 1980)
(Adiba and Delobel, 1977)
(Baldissera et al, 1979)
(Bancilhon and Spyratos, 1981)
(Clemons, 1978)
(Keller and Ullman, 1984)
(Klug, 1979)
(Leavenworth, 1981)
(Navathe and Schkolnick, 1978)
(Roussopoulos, 1982)
(Shmueli and Itai, 1984)

(Yao et al, 1982d)
(Zaniolo, 1979)

DATA DICTIONARY SYSTEMS

Data dictionary systems

(Allen et al, 1982)
(Baker, 1983)
(BCS/DDSWP, 1977)
(BCS/DDSWP, 1982)
(Davenport, 1980)
(FIPS/DDS, 1983a)
(FIPS/DDS, 1983b)
(Hotaka, 1982)
(Kahn and Lumsden, 1983)
(Leon-Hong and Plagman, 1982)
(Loomis et al, 1981)
(Schreiber and Martella, 1979)
(Symons and Tijsma, 1982)
(Van Duyn, 1982)
(Windsor, 1980)

METHODOLOGIES AND REFERENCE MODELS

Information systems design methodologies and evaluation

(Alavi, 1984)
(Bachman and Ross, 1982)
(BCS/ISADWP, 1984)
(Bouzeghoub, 1983)
(Ganguli, 1984)
(Hainaut, 1981)
(Leonard and Luong, 1981)
(Macdonald and Palmer, 1982)
(Maddison et al, 1982)
(Meyer and Schneider, 1979)
(Olle, 1983)
(Olle et al, 1982)
(Olle et al, 1983)
(Somogyi, 1981)

Database design methodologies, methods and techniques

(Agosti, 1983)
(Agosti and Johnson, 1984)
(Agosti et al, 1980)
(Atre, 1980)
(Baker, 1982)
(Bouzeghoub and Valduriez, 1984)
(Brodie and Silva, 1982)
(Ceri, 1983)
(Ceri and Paolini, 1980)
(Chen et al, 1982)
(Chilson and Kudlac, 1983)
(DATAID, 1982)
(Davenport, 1979a)
(De Antonellis and Dileva, 1984)
(Favaloro et al, 1980)
(Herman, 1983)
(Hotaka, 1984)
(Hotaka and Tsubaki, 1981)
(Housel et al, 1979)
(Kahn, 1982)
(Malhotra et al, 1981)
(Malkowitz et al, 1981)
(Molina, 1979)
(Schkolnick, 1978)
(Sundgren, 1978)
(Teorey and Fry, 1980)
(Tozer, 1976)
(Vetter and Maddison, 1981)
(Whittington and Tully, 1982)
(Yao et al, 1982b)
(Yeh and Baker, 1977)

Reference models for the database design process

(Agosti, 1982)
(Agosti and Johnson, 1984)
(Hainaut, 1983)

Design of new database architecutes

(Motro, 1984)
(Shepherd and Kerschberg, 1984)
(Tsur and Zaniolo, 1984)

MANAGEMENT OF THE DESIGN

Computer aided database design

(Batini et al, 1980)
(Ceri, 1983)
(Chen et al, 1982)
(DATAID, 1984)
(Ferrara and Batini, 1984)
(Gerritsen, 1982)
(Hubbard, 1982)
(Irani et al, 1979)
(Katz, 1983)
(March and Severance, 1978)
(Raver and Hubbard, 1977)
(Rolland, 1983)
(Sarda and Isaac, 1981)
(Spiegler, 1983)
(Yao et al, 1982c)

Database restructuring, reorganisation and conversion

(Adiba et al, 1976)
(Bryce, 1981)
(Fry and Teorey, 1978)
(Navathe, 1980)
(Navathe and Fry, 1976)
(Shneidermann and Thomas, 1982)
(Sockut and Goldberg, 1982)
(Su and Lin, 1977)
(Swartwout, 1977)
(Wilson, 1979)
(Wilson, 1980)

DISTRIBUTED DESIGN

Distributed database design

(Adiba et al, 1977)
(Ceri et al, 1981b)
(Champine et al, 1980)
(Chan et al, 1983)
(Davenport, 1981)
(Fitzgerald et al, 1982)
(Kerschberg et al, 1980)
(Mohan and Poposcu-Zeletin, 1982)
(Parent, 1981)

(Rolland and Richard, 1980)
(Symons and Tijsma, 1982)
(Taylor, 1980)
(Teorey and Fry, 1982)

STANDARDS

Relevant standards

(Bachman and Ross, 1982)
(Brodie and Schmidt, 1981)
(Bryce, 1981)
(CCA, 1982)
(desJardin, 1981)
(GAO, 1979)
(Gardarin, 1979)
(ISO, 1981)
(ISO, 1982)
(Mohan and Poposcu-Zeletin, 1982)
(OSI, 1981)
(OSI, 1982)
(Popescu-Zeletin and Weber, 1980)
(Ries, 1982)
(SECT/IEEE, 1982)
(Steel, 1975)
(Steel, 1982)
(Tsichritzis and Klug, 1978)
(Yormark, 1977)
(Zimmermann, 1980)

ANSI/X3/SPARC

(Bachman and Ross, 1982)
(Brodie and Schmidt, 1981)
(De et al, 1981)
(Gardarin, 1979)
(Jardine, 1977)
(Mohan and Popescu-Zeletin, 1982)
(Olle, 1978)
(Steel, 1975)
(Tsichritzis and Klug, 1978)
(Yormark, 1977)

REFERENCES IN ALPHABETICAL ORDER

(Abrial, 1974) J.R. Abrial. Data Semantics. In: DB Management. J.W. Klimbie and K.L. Koffeman (Eds), North-Holland, Amsterdam, Netherlands, 1974, pp.1-60.

A general model for defining database semantics is introduced in this paper.
This has been a seminal paper and it remains a very influential one.

(Adiba, 1980) M. Adiba. Derived Relations: A Unified Mechanism for Views, Snapshots and Distributed Data. IBM Res. Rep. RJ2881, IBM Res. Lab. San Jose, CA, Aug 80, pp.30 (also in Proc. 7th Int. Conf. on VLDB, Cannes, France, Sept 81, pp.293-305).

The unified mechanism called DEREL to define relations in a database and to derive any ralations from a set of relations is described in this report.

(Adiba et al, 1976) M. Adiba, C. Delobel, M. Leonard. A Unified Approach for Modelling Data in Logical Data Base Design. In: (Nijssen, 1976a), pp.311-338.

The problem of conversion from network or hierarchical data structure into relational is addressed in this paper. From the relational schema which is the result of this conversion, the redundant relations are removed and it is derived a set of relations in third normal form.

(Adiba and Delobel, 1977) M. Adiba, C. Delobel. The Problem of the Co-operation Between Different DBMS. In: (Nijssen, 1977a), pp.165-186.

The description of a global view of several databases is

addressed in this paper. The authors believe that this problem has some analogies with the problem of defining a conceptual schema and they propose a methodological approach to the design of a cooperation system of different DBMS.

(Adiba and Lindsay, 1980) M.E. Adiba, B.G. Lindsay. Database Snapshots. IBM Res. Rep. RJ2772, IBM Res. Lab. San Jose, CA, Mar 80, pp.16.

The notion of database snapshot is introduced in this report. A snapshot reflects selected portions of the database so as to allow applications to view the database 'as of' a specific time without having to execute a query at the same specific time. The authors discuss snapshots semantics and implementation.

(Agosti, 1982) M. Agosti. The Necessity of a Reference Model for the Database Design Process. Rep. No.TP-CS-MA-8201, School of Mathematics Statistics and Computing, Thames Polytechnic, London, England, Jul 82, pp.7.

The problem of comparability of database design methods and techniques is stated in this report. The necessity of a reference model for the database design process is underlined.

(Agosti, 1983) M. Agosti. Strategy for a Data System Design Methodology. Rep. No.TP-CS-MA-8302, School of Mathematics Statistics and Computing, Thames Polytechnic, London, England, Dec 83, pp.43.

The database design process is constituted by two distinct abstractions: the data system design and the management design. This report presents the first attempt of specification of the requirements a data system design methodology has to comply with in order to fully support the design process.

(Agosti and Johnson, 1984) M. Agosti, R.G. Johnson. A Framework of Reference for Database Design. DATA BASE, Vol.15, No.4, Summer 84, pp.3-9.

A general framework of reference for DB design is introduced in this paper. The actions which are necessary to implement a DB are divided in two categories: data system design and management design. The utility of a reference model for the data system design is shown.

This framework is being used as a basic block for a general set of requirements for a data system design methodology (Agosti, 1983).

(Agosti et al, 1980) M. Agosti, F. Dalla Libera, F. Lestuzzi, R. Locatelli. Dall'analisi del sistema informativo alla progettazione delle basi di dati. AICA '80 Conf., Bologna, Italy, Oct 80, pp.1364-1373.

The paper deals with the definition of the enterprise schema using a new method that integrates the ISAC (Information System work and Analysis of Changes) and E/R Entity-Relationship) approaches. This new method consists of five steps leading to the E/R schema as final output. The E/R subschemas are defined using the ISAC documents (C-graphs, process tables, I-graphs, A-graphs).

(Alavi, 1984a) M. Alavi. The Evolution of Information Systems Development Approach: Some Field Observations. DATA BASE, Vol.15, No.3, Spring 84, pp.19-24.

The prototyping approach to information systems development is studied in this paper.
The author has studied twelve information systems development projects where prototyping was used. The conclusion of the author is that is present a potential risk in the use of prototyping. Therefore it seems advisable to use prototyping in conjunction and not as a substitute for the systems development life cycle approach.

(Alavi, 1984b) M. Alavi. An Assessment of the Prototyping Approach to Information Systems Development. Comm. of the ACM, Vol.27, No.6, Jun 84, pp.556-563.

The traditional "life cycle" approach and the prototyping approach to information systems development are compared in this work. This is the first work that attack the comparison in a complete way.
The results of this research are valuable also for the database designer because they suggest the usefulness of prototyping. Consequently the integration of the prototyping approach in the DB design process would be studied and experimented.

(Allen et al, 1982) F.W. Allen, M.E.S. Loomis,
M.V. Mannino. The Integrated Dictionary/Directory
System. Computing Surv., Vol.14, No.2, Jun 82,
pp.245-286.

The concept of an integrated Dictionary/Directory System is
discussed in detail, and the state of current systems for
centralised and distributed databases is surveyed.

(Amble et al, 1979) T. Amble, K. Bratbergsengen,
O. Risnes. ASTRAL: A Structured and Unified
Approach to Data Base Design and Manipulation. In:
DB Archit.. G. Bracchi and G.M. Nijssen (Eds),
North-Holland, Amsterdam, Netherlands, 1979,
pp.257-274.

ASTRAL (A STructured Relational Application Language) is a
programming language based on PASCAL, designed for definition
and manipulation of relational databases.

(Atre, 1980) S. Atre. Data Base: Structured
Techniques for Design, Performance, and Management.
Wiley, New York, NY, 1980, pp.xvi+442.

This book demonstrates the principles for designing a
database; it addresses the roles of the different
users/designers categories.
A case study approach has been adopted; a case study for
designing a database for a banking environment is carried
through from the beginning to the end of the book.

(Bachman and Daya, 1977) C.W. Bachman, M. Daya
The Role Concept in Data Models. Proc. 3rd Int
Conf. on VLDB, Tokyo, Japan, Oct 77, pp.464-476.

The data model 'role model' is described in this paper. It
permits the representation of the different roles which a real
world entity may play.
This data model is an extention of the network model.

(Bachman and Ross, 1982) C.W. Bachman, R.G. Ross
Toward a More Complete Reference Model of
Computer-Based Information Systems. Computers and
Standards, Vol.1, 1982, pp.35-48.

ISO/TC97 is the technical committee of the International
Organization for Standardization which is responsible for

computers and information systems. The authors of this paper
believe that the development of a larger reference model than
the ISO/OSI (see (desJardins, 1981), (OSI, 1981), (OSI, 1982),
and (Zimmermann, 1980)) to cover the complete scope of
computer-based information systems would provide an even
greater force within TC97 to assist it in determining the
standards to be produced and to help place existing standards
into a larger context.

(Baker,   1982) G.J.   Baker   (Ed).   Data Analysis
Update.   Database Specialist Group, The British
Computer Society, London, England, 1982, pp.viii+258
(Proc. of BCS Database 82, Thames Polytechnic,
London, England, Apr 82).

The five more known and used data analysis methodologies are
illustrated (ICL, LBMS, IBM, BIS and DMW). Data analysis and
database design experience is presented as well.

(Baker, 1983) G.J.   Baker (Ed).   Data Dictionary
Update.   Database Specialist Group, The British
Computer Society, London, England, 1983, pp.viii+150
(Proc. of BCS Database 83, Thames Polytechnic,
London, England, Apr 83).

This publication contains the papers which were presented at
the BCS Database 83 Conference.
The first part of the volume consists of presentations of data
dictionary software products: IBM DB/DC Data Dictionary, ICL
DDS, TSI Data Catalogue 2, and Cullinane IDD.
The second part consists of presentations on the use and
experience of data dictionary software products at different
organisations.

(Baker and Holloway, 1984) G.J. Baker, S. Holloway
(Eds). Database Design Update. Database Specialist
Group, The British Computer Society, London,
England, 1984, pp.ix+146 (Proc. of BCS Database 84,
Thames Polytechnic, London, England, Apr 84).

This book contains the papers presented at BCS Database 84.
The conference was organised by the BCS Database Specialist
Group and the Thames Polytechnic and held at Dartford Campus
in April 1984. Some papers are pertinent to this bibliography
and are individually referenced.

(Baldissera et al, 1979) C. Baldissera, S. Ceri, G. Pelagatti, G. Bracchi. Interactive Specification and Formal Verification of User's Views in Data Base Design. Proc. 5th Int. Conf. on VLDB, Rio de Janeiro, Brazil, Oct 79, pp.262-272.

This paper describes an interactive methodology for designing user's views starting from the elementary sentences that specify the requirements of the application. The methodology generates a canonical representation, and provides verification algorithms for detecting inconsistencies, redundancies and ambiguities, and for restructuring and optimizing the model.

(Bancilhon and Spyratos, 1981) F. Bancilhon, N. Spyratos. Update Semantics of Relational Views. ACM Trans. on DB Syst., Vol.6, No.4, Dec 81, pp.557-575.

Updates on views must be translated into updates on the underlying database. This paper studies the translation process in the relational model.

(Batini et al, 1980) C. Batini, M. Lenzerini, G. Santucci. A Computer Aided Methodology for Conceptual Data Base Design. AICA '80 Conf., Bologna, Italy, Oct 80, pp.378-397.

This paper describes a system supporting conceptual database design. Incremental enlargements of the conceptual description of user requirements are allowed with top-down and bottom-up procedures. The improvements can involve the data and the transactions.

(BCS/DDSWP, 1977) The British Computer Society Data Dictionary Systems Working Party Report. In: DATA BASE, Vol.9, No.2, Fall 1977 and SIGMOD RECORD, Vol.9, No.4, Dec 77, pp.2-24.

This has been a seminal document for the data dictionary systems (DDS) area. The document reports on the conclusions of the Data Dictionary Systems Working Party of the British Computer Society as of mid-1976. See (BCS/DDSWP, 1982) for the findings of the group as of Summer 82.

(BCS/DDSWP, 1982) The British Computer Society Data Dictionary Systems Working Party. Journal of Development. K.H. Meyer and C.C. Morse (Eds), Summer 82, pp.105.

The Journal of Development presents the DDSWP views on the need for, and facilities provided by, a Data Dictionary System to meet current methods of data processing and foreseeable developments in information technology.

(BCS/ISADWP, 1984) The British Computer Society Information Systems Analysis and Design Working Party. Information Systems Development: A Flexible Framework. R. Maddison (Ed), BCS Database Specialist Group, 1984, pp.154.

This work is the output of a complete rethinking of past approaches to systems development, then it is not its aim to discuss specific IS development and design methodologies. But it proposes a framework for planning, development, and management of information systems.

(Bell, 1984) D.A. Bell. Difficult Data Placement Problems. The Computer Jour., Vol.27, No.4, Nov 84, pp.315-320.

The problems of data placement are studied in this paper. The problems are all concerned with the determination of whether or not a given arrangement of tuples on physical storage is possible.
It is proved to be inadvisable for DB designers to seek algorithms to arrange data in the patterns described, and other systematic approaches, possible with less ambitious goals, are preferable.

(Bell and Deen, 1984) D.A. Bell, S.M. Deen. Hash Trees Versus B-Trees. The Computer Jour., Vol.27, No.3, Aug 84, pp.218-224.

The value of the hash trees method of external hashing as a general indexing technique is assessed in this paper. A comparison with the B-trees method is also presented.
The paper shows that the major scenario in which H-trees provides significant advantages over B-trees is when these is a high traffic of insertions and/or deletions.

(Benci et al, 1976) E. Benci, F. Bodart, H. Bogaert, A. Cabanes. Concepts for the Design of a Conceptual Schema. In: (Nijssen, 1976a), pp.181-200.

The relational model is used as representation model for conceptual schemas. The data structure, the integrity constraints and the evolution rules are represented using the relation concept and the operations on the relations.

(Bhabuta, 1984) L. Bhabuta. Rationale for a New Framework for Information System Development: for the 80's. In: (Baker and Holloway, 1984), pp.39-45.

This article is a brief outline of the work undertaken by the Information Systems Analysis and Design Working Party (ISADWP) of BCS. ISADWP has developed a framework for the planning and development of Information Systems. An outline of the framework is presented with comments on how it addresses the problems of the development.

(Biller and Neuhold, 1977) H. Biller, E.J. Neuhold. Concepts for the Conceptual Schema. In: (Nijssen, 1977a), pp.1-30.

A critical review of data models for a three levels database architecture is presented in this paper. This paper and the (Kershberg et al, 1976) paper can be considered complementary; they review in a complete way the data models situation at that time.

(Biller et al, 1976) H. Biller, W. Gratthaar, E.J. Neuhold. On the Semantics of Data Bases: The Semantics of Data Manipulation Languages. In: (Nijssen, 1976a), pp.239-267.

The semantics of a data manipulation language is formally defined in this paper.

(Boehm et al, 1984) B.W. Boehm, T.E. Gray, T. Seewaldt. Prototyping Versus Specifying: A Multiproject Experiment. IEEE Trans. on Software Engin., Vol.SE-10, No.3, May 84, pp.290-303.

The authors believe that at this time, not enough is known about the relative merits of specifying and prototyping to

reject either approach in favor of the other.
The paper presents a multiproject experiment which provides
some useful quantitative and qualitative information on the
relative effects of the specifying and prototyping approaches.

(Bonfatti et al, 1983) F. Bonfatti, D. Maio, P.
Tiberio. Metodologie di progetto fisico in DBMS
relazionali. Rivista di informatica, Vol.XIII,
No.2, April-June 83, pp.109-126.

This paper addresses a very important physical design problem
for relational DBMS implementations: the secondary indexes
selection.
The selection methods adopted in System-R and in the DATAID
project (see (DATAID, 1982) and (DATAID, 1984)) are presented
and examined in detail.

(Borkin, 1980) S.A. Borkin. Data Models: a
Semantic Approach for Database Systems. The MIT
Press, Cambridge, MA, 1980, pp.xii+269.

This book gives formal definitions of the relevant concepts of
"equivalence" and examples demonstrating the use of the
definitions. As a result concepts as 'data model
equivalence', 'application model equivalence' and 'operation
equivalence' can be defined. This work is mainly concerned
with applying this formal framework to the definition and
study of the equivalence properties of two data models, the
semantic graph data model and the semantic relational data
model.

(Bouzeghoub, 1983) M. Bouzeghoub. Une synthese des
methodes et des outils d'aide a la conception de
systemes d'information. Rapport de Recherche
No.258, INRIA, Centre de Rocquencourt, Le Chesnay,
France, Dec 83, pp.64.

This report presents a critical synthesis of some methods and
tools for information systems design. It distinguishes
between static and dynamic aspects to be addressed during the
design and it divides the analysis of the methods following
this division. The ANSI/SPARC approach is adopted, thus the
conceptual, external and internal levels are addressed.

(Bouzeghoub and Valduriez, 1984) M. Bouzeghoub, P. Valduriez. New Tools for Logical Database Design. In: (Baker and Holloway, 1984), pp.131-141.

This paper reviews the main approaches for describing the static aspects of informatiom systems. Some tools for conceptual and implementation database design are also presented. The authors believe that, once the design has been completed, it is very difficult to integrate new design rules. The expert systems approach is believed to be more adaptable to the changes to be inserted in the design.

(Bowers, 1984) D.S. Bowers. A Database Architecture for Aggregate-Incomplete Data. The Computer Jour., Vol.27, No.4, Nov 84, pp.294-300.

The "aggregate-incomplete" class of data is defined in this paper. Such data are described by "hierarchic attribute sets". The paper shows that, if aggregate values are stored for such data, then the problem of materializing some aggregate values is complicated by the variety of materialization strategies.
The author asserts that it is desirable to store aggregate values if data are incomplete, then an architecture based on a tree structure is proposed for a database to hold aggregate-incomplete data.

(Bracchi et al, 1976) G. Bracchi, P. Paolini, G. Pelagatti. Binary Logical Associations in Data Modelling. In: (Nijssen, 1976a), pp.125-148.

The purpose of this paper is to discuss the most suitable data model at the conceptual schema level. The paper is structured in four main sections: determination of the requirements for the construction of the conceptual schema; development of a logical frame of reference that allows comparison of the different data models; discussion of the network and relational data models; and the final section that is devoted to the presentation of a data model based on Binary Logical Associations (BLA). This data model is usually referred as Binary Data Model.

(Bracchi et al, 1979) G. Bracchi, A. Furtado, G. Pelagatti. Constraint Specification in Evolutionary Data Base Design. In: Formal Models and Practical Tools for Inform. Syst. Design. H.-J. Schneider (Ed), North-Holland, IFIP, 1979, pp.149-165.

This paper discusses the various requirements that should be collected and specified for the database design process, and it shows the relevance of the requirements to the subsequent components of the design process.

(Breutmann et al, 1979) B. Breutmann, E. Falkenberg, R. Mauer. CSL: A language for defining conceptual schemas. In: <u>Data Base Architecture</u>. G. Bracchi and G.M. Nijssen (Eds), North-Holland, 1979, pp.237-255.

This paper describes a high level data definition language, CSL, which provides powerful capabilities for defining conceptual schemas within the three level architecture of DBMS.

(Brodie, 1980) M.L. Brodie. <u>Data Abstraction, Databases, and Conceptual Modelling: An Annotated Bibliography</u>. NBS Special Pub. 500-59, May 80, pp.x+75.

Abstraction, one of the most common and most important intellectual activities, enables people to model and deal with the world around them. This observation is basic to modelling parts of the 'real world' in computers. In light of this the topic of abstraction and its representation has been actively and fruitfully investigated by researchers in computer and information sciences. In particular, the three fields of artificial intelligence, databases, and programming languages have addressed overlapping issues within the area of conceptual models for dynamics systems of complex data. This bibliography is intended to be a comprehensive reference to work on conceptual modelling of dynamic systems of complex data; it covers the temporal span between 1967 and 1980. A second objective is to encourage the cross-fertilisation of the three research areas. Although each area has its own, unique concerns, there are important concepts, goals, and problems common to all three areas. The bibliography emphasises one of these concepts, <u>data abstraction</u>. It is hoped that this bibliography will encourage an exchange of information on the technologies being used to specify and represent conceptual models in each of the areas and on problems that are still to be solved. (from author's preface)

(Brodie, 1981) M.L. Brodie. On Modelling Behavioural Semantics of Databases. <u>Proc. 7th Int. Conf. on VLDB</u>, Cannes, France, Sept 81, pp.32-42.

This paper presents forms of abstraction for behaviour modelling in the context of a semantic data model. Behaviour schemes are presented as aids for behaviour modelling at a gross level of detail. Behaviour specifications are introduced for the precise definition of behavioural properties.

(Brodie, 1982) M.L. Brodie. Axiomatic Definitions for Data Model Semantics. Inform. Syst., Vol.7, No.2, 1982, pp.182-197.

The axiomatic method, a widely accepted technique for the precise definition of programming language semantics, is used to define data model semantics.

(Brodie and Schmidt, 1981) M.L. Brodie, J.W. Schmidt (Eds). Final Report of the ANSI/X3/SPARC DBS-SG Relational Database Task Group. Doc No.SPARC-81-690, Sept 81, pp.iii+62. In: SIGMOD RECORD, Vol.12, No.4, Jul 82.

This report has been compiled by the Relational Task Group (RTG) to support the proposal for a relational standard. I documents the results of the RTG's investigations which consisted of three tasks: 1) identify the fundamental concepts of the Relational Data Model (RDM); 2) characterise the features of existing and potential RDBMS to determine the interface functions; 3) investigate the role of the RDM and RDBMS in a DBMS architectural framework such as the ANSI/X3/SPARC prototypical architecture, and in a coherent family of DBMS standards.
The group has decided the first two tasks were tractable (the results are found in Chap.2 and 3), on the contrary the third task addressed open research problems (Chap.4 documents the problems by identify issues and known alternatives). Chap. summarises the results and proposes guidelines for developing a relational standard.
This report confirms the important tendency in the D management area towards standardisation. Then it could be milestone for RDBMS and it merits a careful reading.

(Brodie and Silva, 1982) M.L. Brodie, E. Silva Active and Passive Component Modelling: ACM/PCM In: (Olle et al, 1982), pp.41-90.

ACM/PCM is a modelling methodology for the design an development of moderate to large size database-intensiv applications. This paper describes the tools and technique for the conceptual database design component.

(Brodie and Zilles, 1980) M.L. Brodie, S.N. Zilles (Eds). Proc. of Workshop on Data Abstraction, Databases and Conceptual Modelling. Pingree Park, Co, Jun 80, pp.vi+211.

This proceedings consists of tutorials, edited transcripts of the workshop sessions and position papers prepared by the partecipants. It is relevant to point out that the workshop was intended as a forum in which artificial intelligence, database and programming language researchers could exchange ideas on conceptual modelling of systems of complex data.

(Brown and Parker, 1983) R. Brown, D.S. Parker. LAURA: A Formal Data Model and her Logical Design Methodology. Proc. 9th Int. Conf. on VLDB, Florence, Italy, Oct-Nov 83, pp.206-218.

This paper describes the LAURA data model and its use in the conceptual design phase of a design methodology.

(Bryce, 1981) M. Bryce (Panel Chairman). Standards. DATA BASE, Voll.12 and 13, No.4 and 1, Summer-Fall 1981, pp.34-38.

The objective of the 'Standards Working Panel' was to recommend standards that a manager should consider when converting data from present sources (manual, semiautomated or automated) to a DBMS. The panel has considered administrative guidelines as well as technical standards, since both are essential to an effective conversion process.
The paper reports the results of the panel as well as a review of the various standards activities in the database area.

(Bubenko, 1977a) J.A. Bubenko. The Temporal Dimension in Information Modeling. In: (Nijssen, 1977a), pp.93-118.

The problem of dealing with time-varying associations or relationships in conceptual information modelling is examined. A conceptual framework where time is treated in an unrestricted fashion is introduced.

(Bubenko,   1977b)   J.A.   Bubenko.   IAM: An
Inferential   Abstract Modeling Approach to Design of
Conceptual Schema. Proc.   ACM-SIGMOD Int.   Conf.
on Management of Data,   Toronto,   Canada, Aug 77,
pp.62-74.

The systematic development of the conceptual schema
specification is addressed in this paper.

(Bubenko, 1979) J.A.   Bubenko.   On the Role of
'Understanding Models' in Conceptual Schema Design.
Proc. 5th Int. Conf. on VLDB, Rio de Janeiro,
Brazil, Oct 79, pp.129-139.

The author suggests that two levels should be considered when
designing a conceptual schema: the 'understanding level' and
the 'conceptual database level'. The first level includes the
study of the set of information requirements and of the
conceptual information model. The second level includes the
conceptual processing models. The paper describes connections
between these four 'objects'.

. (Bubenko, 1981) J.A.   Bubenko.   On Concepts and
Strategies   for   Requirements   and   Information
Analysis. SYSLAB Rep. No.4, Goteborg, Sweden, Feb
81, pp.50.

The present computer based information systems are more
integrated with   the   operations and activities of the
organisation than the computer based IS of   the   past.
Therefore the analysis and definition of requirements are more
complex. This report presents two different approaches of
requirements specification.

(Bubenko et al, 1978) J.A. Bubenko, S.B.   Yao, B.
Sundgren, P. Heyderhoff, I.R. Palmer, J.M. Smith,
M. Theys, J.-M. Plisnier, Panel on Data Base
design.   Proc.   4th Int.   Conf.   on VLDB,
West-Berlin, Germany, Sept 78, pp.1-20.   (also in
Issues in DB Management. H.   Weber and A.I.
Wasserman (Eds), North-Holland, 1979, pp.1-37.)

The introductory paper to the panel on database design by
Bubenko and· Yao, the paper by Sundgren, see also reference
(Sundgren, 1978), and the comments on that paper by John Smith
are grouped here as written documents for the panel. These
documents represent an effort for bridging the gap between the
theory and the practice of database design.

(Carlis et al, 1983) J.V. Carlis, S.T. March, G.W.
Dickson. Physical Database Design: a DSS Approach.
Inform. and Management, Vol.6, No.4, Aug 83,
pp.211-224.

This paper describes how a decision support approach was
applied to the problem of physical database design.

(CCA, 1982) Computer Corporation of America.   An
Architecture for Database Management Standards. NBS
Special Pub. 500-86, Jan 82, pp.v+47.

A proposed architectural framework, developed by the Computer
Corporation of America (CCA), is presented in this report for
review by USA Federal Government data processing personnel,
computer hardware and software vendors, and other interested
groups and individuals.
The complexity of DBMS is represented by an architecture that
classifies functions into components, and identifies both
external and internal interfaces to these components.

(Ceri, 1980) S. Ceri. La progettazione di basi di
dati. Clup, Milano, 1980, pp.106.

This book has been written as lectures notes on database
design.
It is an advanced introduction to the subject; it consists of
an account of the present practice and of the description of a
complete design methodology with an example that uses it.

(Ceri, 1983) S. Ceri (Ed). Methodology and Tools
for Data Base Design. North-Holland, Amsterdam, The
Netherlands, 1983, pp.x+255.

This book describes the results of the first three years of
the DATAID project, a project financed by the Italian Research
Council within a general national computing science project.
The first part of the book describes the DATAID-1 methodology,
a design methodology that covers all the database design
components. The second part of the book describes some
support tools to the DATAID-1 methodology.

(Ceri and Paolini, 1980) S. Ceri, P. Paolini.
Metodologia per il progetto di basi di dati. AICA
'80 Conf., Bologna, Italy, Oct 80, pp.625-641.

A methodology to be used in real world applications (not a

methodology to be used as a research vehicle) is described in
this paper. It integrates tools that are currently used by
designers, but it separates issues dependent on the available
DBMS from the ones that are independent from it.

> (Ceri et al, 1981a) S.   Ceri, G.   Pelagatti, G.
> Bracchi.   Structured   methodology for designing
> static and · dynamic aspects of data   base
> applications.   Inform.   Syst.,   Vol.6,   1981,
> pp.31-45.

This paper describes the design approach of the conceptual
component within the DATAID project, see also (Ceri, 1983).

> (Ceri et al, 1981b) S.   Ceri, S.   Navathe, G.
> Wiederhold.   Optimal   Design   of   Distributed
> Databases. Rep. No.STAN-CS-81-884, Dept.   of
> Computer Science, Stanford Univ., Dec 81, pp.47.

An optimisation model for a non-redundant allocation of the
database is presented in this report. The inputs required for
the distribution design phase are: an enterprise schema, a
tabulation of transaction and their volume, distribution
requirements.
The paper is pertinent to this bibliography because of the
definition of the context in which a solution of the database
allocation is proposed.

> (Champine et al, 1980) G.A. Champine, R.D.   Coop,
> R.C.   Heinselman. Distributed Computer Systems
> Impact on Management, Design and Analysis.
> North-Holland, Amsterdam, the Netherlands, 1980,
> pp.xvi+380.

The scope of this book is to provide an overview of the area
of distributed computer systems.   It is pertinent to this
bibliography because it addresses the design of DDE
introducing a general design methodology. It is also valuable
because it constructs connections between different areas
involved in distributed computer systems that are important
for the DB designer.

> (Chan et al, 1982) A. Chan, S. Danberg, S.   Fox,
> W.K. Lin, A. Nori, D. Ries. Storage and Access
> Structures to Support a Semantic Data Model. Proc.
> 8th Int. Conf. on VLDB, Mexico City, Mexico, Sep
> 82, pp.122-130.

A set of storage and access structures for supporting a semantic data model are presented in this paper. Prominent features of this data model include the notions of generalisation hierarchies and referential constraints.

(Chan et al, 1983) A. Chan, U. Dayal, S. Fox, D. Ries. Supporting a Semantic Data Model in a Distributed Database System. Proc. 9th Int. Conf. on VLDB, Florence, Italy, Oct-Nov 83, pp.354-363.

This paper describes an implementation approach for supporting logical pointers between distributed entities. This approach is being employed in a DDBMS that supports a semantic data model.

(Chen, 1976) P.P. Chen. The Entity-Relationship Model - Toward a Unified View of Data. ACM Trans. on DB Syst., Vol.1, No.1, Mar 76, pp.9-36.

The milestone paper that introduces and defines the entity-relationship data model. The model incorporates some of the important semantic information of the real world. A special diagrammatic technique is introduced as a tool for DB design.

(Chen, 1982) P.P. Chen. Applications of the Entity-Relationship Model. In: (Yao et al, 1982a), pp.87-113.

(Chen and Yao, 1977) P.P. Chen, S.B. Yao. Design and Performance Tools for Data Base Systems. Proc. 3rd Int. Conf. on VLDB, Tokyo, Japan, Oct 77, pp.3-15.

Tools for conceptual, implementation and physical database design are reviewed in this paper. These tools are classified and their features are compared.

(Chen et al, 1982) P.P. Chen, I. Chung, D. Perry. Survey of State-of-the-Art Logical Database Design Tools. Rep. No.NBS-GCR-82-389, Washington, DC, Apr 82, pp.vii+87.

A survey of the state of the art of logical database design tools is presented in this report. The survey is concentrated on the conceptual component of the database design process, then tools for the requirements design and for the implementation and physical design are not included.

(Chilson and Kudlac, 1983) D.W. Chilson, M.E. Kudlac. Database Design: a Survey of Logical and Physical Design Techniques. DATA BASE, Vol.15, No.1, Fall 83, pp.11-19.

This paper presents a study on techniques presently available to assist in the process of database design.

(Christodoulakis, 1984) S. Christodoulakis. Implications of Certain Assumptions in Database Performance Evaluation. ACM Trans. on DB Syst., Vol.9, No.2, Jun 84, pp.163-186.

The assumptions of uniformity and independence of attribute values, random placement of the qualifying records among the blocks of a file, and uniformity of queries are often used in actual database environments. The author shows that when these assumptions are not satisfied, large errors in the estimation of performance may result. Applications in physical database design and in query optimisation are also discussed.

(Clemons, 1978) E.K. Clemons. An External Schema Facility to Support Data Base Update. In: Databases: Improving Usability and Responsiveness. B. Shneiderman (Ed), Academic Press, New York, NY, 1978, pp.371-398.

(Codd, 1970) E.F. Codd. A Relational Model of Data for Large Shared Data Banks. Comm. of the ACM, Vol.13, No.6, Jun 70, pp.377-387.

This is the original Codd's paper on the relational approach. It can be considered a foundation-stone of the database management area; in fact it introduces the reletional data model and clarify the importance of data independence.
"Historical" note: this paper is inserted in the information retrieval (IR) section of the issue of Communications of the ACM; in fact at that time database management was still included in IR.

(Codd, 1979) E.F. Codd. Extending the Database Relational Model to Capture More Meaning. ACM Trans. on DB Syst., Vol.4, No.4, Dec 79, pp.397-434.

Extentions to the relational model to support certain atomic and molecular semantics are proposed in this paper. These extentions represent a synthesis of many ideas from the previous published work in semantic modeling plus the introduction of new rules for insertion, update, and deletion, as well as new algebraic operators.

(Colombetti et al, 1978) M. Colombetti, P. Paolini, G. Pelagatti. Nondeterministic Languages Used for the definition of Data Models. In: Logic and Data Bases. H. Gallaire and J. Minker (Eds), Plenum Press, New York, NY, 1978, pp.237-257.

The main purpose of this paper is to show the practical possibility of using algebraic equations for the definition of data models for data bases. The definition of a model based on binary ralations is given. The algebraic equations that define the data model are translated into PROLOG clauses. The obtained implementation makes possible the automated testing of the equations.

(Cookson, 1983) M.J. Cookson. Taxonomic Studies on Current Approaches to Systems Analysis. The Computer Jour., Short Note, Vol.26, No.3, Aug 83, pp.283-284.

The taxonomy for current approaches to systems analysis presented in (Wood-Harper and Fitzgerald, 1982) is examined in this paper. Some changes are proposed and a major problem of such classification method is identified.

(Couger et al, 1982) J.D. Couger, M.A. Colter, R.W. Knapp. Advanced System Development/Feasibility Techniques. Wiley, New York, NY, 1982, pp.xiii+506.

This book is following the 1974 book entitled 'System Analysis Techniques' by Couger as editor. The 1974 book has been the first volume to gather the landmark papers for the MIS discipline to demonstrate the theoretical basis of the system development techniques for business applications of the computer.
The present book contains an expanded classification of the

techniques in the field. It also includes landmark papers published since the publication of the first volume.

(Curtice and Jones, 1982) R.M. Curtice, P.E. Jones Jr. Logical Data Base Design. Van Nostrand Reinhold, New York, NY, 1982, pp.xii+227.

The emphasis of this book is on the practical aspects of the conceptual database design component. The examples are very helpful because they illustrate how the authors' approach yields a conceptual database design.

(DATAID, 1982) Obiettivo DATAID. Metodologia manuale DATAID-1 (Versione 1): Descrizione sintetica. CNR, Progetto Finalizzato Informatica, Sottoprogetto P2, Obiettivo DATAID, 1982.

This document contains a synthetic description of the DATAID-1 methodology of database design. See (Ceri, 1983) for a complete documentation on it. The tools that have been developed to support the designer using DATAID-1 are presented in (DATAID, 1984).

(DATAID, 1984) Obiettivo DATAID. Proc. of the Conf. La progettazione di basi di dati assistita da calcolatore. Italian Research Council (CNR) and AICA, Roma, Italy, Apr 84.

These proceedings present the computer aided database design tools that have been developed by the DATAID team of the national computing science project of the Italian Research Council. These tools support the different components of the database design process.
The NLDA and the CATRA tools can be used during the information requirements design, if they are adopted they have to be used in sequence: 1) NLDA (Natural Language Design Aid) permits the user to express the requirements in Italian; the tool implements the sintactic and the semantic analysis of the requirements; 2) CATRA (Computer Aided Tool for Requirements Analysis) collects the requirements in a coherent set; it builds the data, operations and events glossaries.
Three tools have been developed for the conceptual database design; the designer can choose one of these: ISTDA, INCOD-DTE or DIALOGO; the choice of one of these tools is depending on the preference of the designer for the tool and for the output generated by the tool; in fact DIALOGO produces a full conceptual schema using the semantic GALILEO model; ISTDA (Interactive Schema and Transaction Definition

Aid) generates the conceptual schema in an "enriched" entity-relationship model; INCOD-DTE (INteractive Conceptual Design of Data, Transactions, Events) produces the representation of the static and dynamic requirements using the binary data model.

Two tools have been developed for the implementation design component: 1) EASYMAP-SIST that implements a relational schema for a conceptual schema; 2) ISIDE (Integrated System for Implementation DEsign) that transforms a conceptual schema in a CODASYL schema.

Another tool have been developed, it is named EOS and it can be used to simulate real operations of a database corresponding to an implementation schema of a specific application; this tool evaluates the execution time of different database operations in different situations of the host computer system.

(Date, 1981a) C.J. Date. An Introduction to Database Systems. 3rd Ed. Addison-Wesley, Reading, MA, 1981, pp.xxviii+574.

This is the third edition of the Date's introductory book on databases. This edition contains the basic material on the subject, the advanced material has been transferred in a supplemental volume. As the previous edition it is one of the most readable introduction to DBMS.

(Date, 1981b) C.J. Date. Referential Integrity. Proc. 7th Int. Conf. on VLDB, Cannes, France, Sept 81, pp.2-12.

Referential integrity is discussed in this paper in general and in detail in the relational framework.

(Davenport, 1978) R.A. Davenport. Data Analysis for Database Design. The Australian Computer Jour., Vol.10, No.4, Nov 78, pp.122-137.

The primary purpose of data analysis is defined to be the determination of the fundamental nature of an organisation's data resources and the organisation and documentation of all relevant facts concerning this data. The author describes a methodology for data analysis. When this methodology is used in preparation for database design, it involves the two phases: entity analysis and functional analysis.

(Davenport, 1979a) R.A. Davenport. Logical Database Design - From Entity Model to DBMS Structure. The Australian Computer Jour., Vol.11, No.3, Aug 79, pp.82-97.

A methodology for the conceptual database design component is presented in this paper. The methodology has been applied to a sample environment and produced a number of possible DB structures for the TOTAL DBMS.

(Davenport, 1979b) R.A. Davenport. The Application of Data Analysis - Experience with the Entity-Relationship Approach. Proc. 1st Int. Conf. on E/R Approach to Syst. Analysis and Design. Los Angeles, CA, Dec 79, pp.463-481.

This paper is concentrated on the practical problems that arise when undertaking data analysis and the solutions which have been found to be successful in the author's experience.

(Davenport, 1980) R.A. Davenport. Data Administration - the Need for a New Function. In: Inform. Processing 80, S.H. Lavington (Ed). North-Holland, 1980, pp.505-510.

(Davenport, 1981) R.A. Davenport. Design of distributed data base systems. The Computer Jour., Vol.24, No.1, 1981, pp.31-41.

This paper outlines the alternative structures available to the designer of a distributed database system and examines the viability of these structures. In addition some of the problems which are unique to distributed systems are examined.

(Davis, 1981) G.B. Davis. Strategies for Information Requirements Determination. MISRC-WP-82-02, University of Minnesota, Minneapolis, MN, Sept 81, pp.45.

This article identifies two major levels of requirements: the organisational information requirements (for a planned portfolio of applications and the detailed information requirements (to be used for a specific application).
Different strategies for collecting information requirements are introduced and a contingency approach for selecting one of these strategies is given.

(Davis and Coumpas, 1984) R.H Davis, P. Coumpas. A Dynamic File Organization Model. The Computer Jour., Vol.27, No.2, May 84, pp.143-150.

A dynamic analytical file organisation model is presented. This model enables the file designer to estimate file performance and cost against time and offers a quantitative solution to file organisation problems. This approach is not found in models previously studied.

(DDBWG/BCS, 1983) DDBWG/BCS. Initial Report of The Distributed Database Working Group of The British Computer Society. D.A. Hickman (Ed). DDBWG/BCS, London, England, 1983, pp.82.

This report provides guidance to those managers and designers who are faced with design decisions where the options include storage of master data at several nodes of a network.

(De et al, 1981) P. De, W.D. Haseman, Y.H. So. Four-schema approach: an extended model for database architecture. Inform. Syst., Vol.6, No.2, 1981, pp.117-124.

The authors propose a four-schema architecture as an overall design framework, extending the ANSI/X3/SPARC three-schema architecture. They have split up the conceptual schema into two components - the 'enterprise schema' and the 'canonical schema'.

(De Antonellis and Dileva, 1984) V. De Antonellis, A. Dileva. Tutorial 3: Database Design Methodology. Tutorial Notes, IEEE Computer Society, 1984, pp.52.

This tutorial presents the main features of the DATAID-1 database design methodology which has been developed as part of the DATAID project. See (Ceri, 1983), (DATAID, 1982) and (DATAID, 1984) for other references on the project and on the methodology.
In this work main features of DATAID-1 are discussed with resect of other approaches. A case study related to a banking environment is described.

(De Antonellis and Zonta, 1981) V. De Antonellis,
B. Zonta. Modelling Events in Data Base
Applications Design. Proc. 7th Int. Conf. on
VLDB, Cannes, France, Sept 81, pp.23-31.

The description of dynamics in the design of applications that
use the database technology are investigated in this paper. A
formalism for events description is proposed and its
utilisation is presented.

(Deen, 1980) S.M. Deen. A canonical schema for a
generalised data model with local interfaces. The
Computer Jour., Vol.23, No.3, 80, pp.201-206.

A global schema is proposed for a generalised database system
capable of supporting interfaces to other systems, e.g.
relational or network; the notion of this global schema is
based on a canonical data model.

(Deen and Hammersley, 1980) S.M. Deen, P.
Hammersley (Eds). Proc. Int. Conf. on Data
Bases. Univ. of Aberdeen, Scotland, Jul 80. BCS
Workshop Series. Heyden, London, England, 1980,
pp.xii+288.

Several papers presented at the conference are pertinent to
this bibliography, then they are individually referenced by
the name of the first author.

(Delobel, 1980) C. Delobel. An Overview of the
Relational Data Theory. In: Inform. Processing
80. S.H. Lavington (Ed). North-Holland, 1980,
pp.413-426.

The concepts of the relational data theory for database are
reviewed in this paper. Special attention is paid to the
basic problems such as manipulation of dependencies, schema
equivalence, and methods for designing a relational schema.

(Demo and Marini, 1980) B. Demo, G. Marini
Principi e strumenti per l'organizzazione de
requisiti degli utenti di basi di dati. AICA '8
Conf., Bologna, Italy, Oct 80, pp.654-663.

A study of the information requirements formulation an
analysis phase of the database design process.

(desJardins, 1981) R. desJardins. Overview and Status of the ISO Reference Model of Open Systems Interconnection. Computer Networks, Vol.5, No.2, Apr 81, pp.77-80.

This paper gives a general introduction to the ISO Reference Model of Open Systems Interconnection (OSI). The status of the OSI Reference Model is as at the end of 1980.

(dos Santos et al, 1979) C.S. dos Santos, E.J. Neuhold, A.L. Furtado. A data type approach to the Entity-Relationship model. Proc. Int. Conf. on E/R Approach to Syst. Analysis and Design, Dec 79, Los Angeles, CA, pp.114-130.

Database semantics is considered with a data type approach, using the Entity-Relationship model as a framework.

(El-Masri and Wiederhold, 1979) R. El-Masri, G. Wiederhold. Data Model Integration Using the Structural Model. Proc. ACM-SIGMOD Int. Conf. on Management of Data, Boston, MA, May-Jun 79, pp.191-202.

The authors address the problem of view integration when user data models are expressed using the structural model; the structural model is built from relations in Boyce-Codd normal form. They show how to integrate different representations of two related real-world entity class.

(Falkenberg, 1976) E. Falkenberg. Concepts for Modelling Information. In: (Nijssen, 1976a), pp.95-109.

A method for modelling information is proposed which is based on two basic concepts, object and role. This is the object-role model; its application is illustrated.

(Falkenberg, 1980) E. Falkenberg. On the conceptual approach to data bases. In: (Deen and Hammersley, 1980), pp.92-98.

The author identifies some criteria and principles essential to the conceptual approach to data bases. The most essential issue of the conceptual approach is the conceptual schema and its design, thus the paper is mainly focused on it.

(Favaloro et al, 1980) E.   Favaloro, L.   Sassone
Corsi, E.   Sassone Corsi.   Applicazione pratica e
messa a punto di un approccio sistematico di data
base design.   AICA '80 Conf., Bologna, Italy, Oct
80, pp.398-403.

A database design approach that is used by the "Systems and
Management" company is presented.

(Ferrara and Batini, 1984) F.M.   Ferrara, C.
Batini.   GDOC: A Tool for Computerized Design and
Documentation of Database Systems.   DATA   BASE,
Vol.15, No.4, Summer 84, pp.15-20.

Release 2.1 of GDOC, a tool for computer aided design of
database applications, is described in this paper.
GDOC provides for the interactive specification of the
conceptual schema of the application, expressed in an enriched
entity-relationship model and produces relevant documentation.
Moreover, GDOC generates the physical DB and the operating
programs in a dBASE II environment.

(Finkelstein et al, 1982) S.J.   Finkelstein, M
Schkolnick, P.   Tiberio.   DBDSGN - A Physical
Database Design Tool for System R. Database Engin.
Mar 82, pp.9-11.

This paper describes an automatic tool for the design of the
physical component of a database which has to be implemented
with System R.

(FIPS/DDS, 1983a) P.A. Konig, A.   Goldfine, J.J
Newton (Eds). Functional Specifications for
Federal   Information   Processing   Standard   Dat
Dictionary System (FIPS/DDS).   National Bureau o
Standards Rep. No.NBSIR 82-2619, Washington, DC
Jan 83.

This interim report contains functional specifications for the
basic functions that data dictionary software must perform t
satisfy federal agency requirements.   The functionalit
specified will be incorporated into a planned Federa
Information Processing Standard (FIPS) Data Dictionary Syste
(DDS).

(FIPS/DDS, 1983b) Federal Information Processing Standard for Data Dictionary Systems. Vol.1: General Description of the FIPS DDS; Vol.2: Command Language Interface Specifications; Vol.3: Interactive Interface Descriptions; Vol.4: Dictionary Administrator Support Specifications. Institute for Computer Sciences and Technology, National Bureau of Standards, Washington, DC, Aug 83.

CST of NBS is developing a Data Dictionary System as an bjective of the Federal Information Processing Standards rogram. The FIPS DDS is a planned product in a family of tandards and guidelines for data management software and ractices that ICST is developing. The FIPS DDS will be a oftware specification which Federal Agencies may use in the valuation and selection of DDS's.

(Fitzgerald et al, 1982) G. Fitzgerald, J.O. Jefferys, J. Kerridge, W. Pilgrim, H.M. Robinson, G.M. Stacey. A Reference Model and Abstract Syntax for Distributed Database Systems. Proc. of 2nd British Nat. Conf. on DB, Bristol, England, Jul 82, pp.133-146.

(Frost, 1983) R.A. Frost. SCHEMAL: Yet Another Conceptual Schema Definition Language. The Computer Jour., Vol.26, No.3, Aug 83, pp.228-234.

new conceptual schema definition language, called SCHEMAL, s presented in this paper. This language can be used to dentify inconsistencies in the user's view of the pertinent art of the information system the user is interested, and to utomatically maintain the semantic integrity of the database.

(Fry and Teorey, 1978) J.P. Fry, T.J. Teorey. Design and Performance Tools for Improving Database Usability and Responsiveness. In: Databases: Improving Usability and Responsiveness. B. Shneiderman (Ed), Academic Press, New York, NY, 1978, pp.151-189.

ne authors believe that the main problem facing the DB dministrator is how to use DBMS effectively. In order to ddress this problem, it is generally agreed that the DB dministrator needs design tools at each step in the ife-cycle to perform his function effectively. The authors ntroduce a framework of the data-based development and

operation cycle to survey various tools which are currently
being developed in the research environment.
The authors propose a DB design and implementation laboratory
as a means of developing and implementing strategies to allow
independently developed computer based design aids and problem
specification methodologies to be integrated into a
comprehensive, coordinated design system.

(Gallaire et al, 1984) H. Gallaire, J. Minker
J.-M. Nicolas. Logic and Databases: A Deductive
Approach. Computer Surv., Vol.16, No.2, Jun 84, pp
153-185.

Logic as it is applied to databases is the subject of thi
survey paper. Some specific themes of DB design are
addressed, such as the data dependencies theme. The secon
part of the survey deals with the general problem of th
representation and manipulation of deduced facts an
incomplete information.

(Ganguli, 1984) D. Ganguli. Information Managemen
Using a Relational Database. In: (Baker an
Holloway, 1984), pp.97-130.

The ADR (Applied Data Research) system design methodology i
presented in this paper. In this methodology, a Relationa
Information System Design starts using the results of
strategic DP plan (this plan covers four areas: th
organisational units of the enterprise, the functions withi
these units, the sources of data necessary to carry out th
functions, the information entities). An example is reporte
in the paper. The methodology presented here has bee
extended by ADR to incorporate a migration plan from existin
VSAM and DL/1 systems to a new system under ADR/DATACOM/D
software.

(GAO, 1979) United States General Accounting Office
Data Base Management Systems -- Without Carefu
Planning There Can Be Problems. Report To Th
Congress of the United States by the Comptrolle
General. Jun 79, pp.ix+48.

This report has been compiled by the United States Genera
Accounting Office (GAO) to survey the usage of the DBM
technology in the Federal agencies and to make recommendatior
for future actions in the area.

(Gardarin,   1979)   G.   Gardarin.   A   unified
architecture for data and message management. Proc.
of the Nat. Computer Conf., 1979, pp.681-688.

(Gerritsen, 1982) R.   Gerritsen.   Tools for the
Automation of Database Design.   In: (Yao et al,
1982a), pp.72-86.

(Gross et al, 1980) J.M.   Gross, P.E.   Jackson, J.
Joyce, F.A.   McGuire. Distributed Database Design
and Administration. In: Distributed Data Bases.
I.W.   Draffan and F. Poole (Eds). Cambridge Univ.
Press, England, 1980, pp.285-322.

This paper deals with the techniques required to design and
implement a DDB system.
The authors regard simulation and performance testing as vital
phases in the development of any DDB, particularly because the
complexity of a DDB renders it less amenable to calculation
methods than conventional DBs.
This paper has been presented at Sheffield in 1979 and some
expressed considerations are inevitably time-dependent.

(Hackett, 1981) J.E. Hackett. Data Analysis.   SPL
International, London, England, Apr 81, pp.14.

(Hainaut, 1981) J.L.   Hainaut.   Theoretical and
Practical Tools for Data Base Design. Proc. 7th
Int. Conf. on VLDB, Cannes, France, Sept 81,
pp.216-224.

The author briefly presents the Information System Design
Approach under development at the`Institut d'Informatiquè of
the University of Namur, Belgium, which proposes a four steps
design process.   The paper mainly concerns with techniques
which may be useful for a large range of schema transformation
methods.   The tools presented consist of two families of
reversible mappings on binary structures. The binary model is
considered as a particular case of a gereralised relational
model. Consequently, the transformations are valid for other
models such as Codd's and E/R models, considered as particular
cases of the generalised model.

(Hainaut, 1983) J.L. Hainaut. Cadre de reference pour la conception de bases de donnees. Institut d'Informatique, Facultes universitaires N.D. de la paix, Namur, Belgium, Dec 83.

This document defines a logical framework for the design of a database. In particular it addresses the design process from the conceptual component to the physical component. It can be used as a reference model for the analysis of database design methods and techniques.

(Hall et al, 1976) P. Hall, J. Owlett, S. Todd. Relations and Entities. In: (Nijssen, 1976a), pp.201-220.

The entity model and the relational data model are considered as candidates for their use in the conceptual schema. The paper shows how the advantages of both can be integrated in one system. The irriducible relations and their use in the conceptual schema are also discussed.

(Hawryszkiewycz, 1980) I.T. Hawryszkiewycz. Alternate Implementations of the Conceptual Schema. Inform. Syst., Vol.5, 1980, pp.203-217.

The author proposes that rather than using one data model at the conceptual level, it is better to provide the database administrator with a set of facilities to be used to define arbitrary data models in the conceptual component.

(Heitmeyer and McLean, 1983) C.L. Heitmeyer, J.D. McLean. Abstract Requirements Specification: A New Approach and Its Application. IEEE Trans. on Software Engin., Vol.SE-9, No.5, Sept 83, pp.580-589.

An abstract requirements specification states system requirements precisely without describing a real or a paradigm implementation. This paper introduces an approach to produce abstract requirements specifications that applies to a significant class of real world systems.
The paper introduces some formalisms that can be useful for abstract database design.

(Herman, 1983) M. Herman. A Database Design
Methodology for an Integrated Database Environment.
DATA BASE, Vol.15, No.1, Fall 83, pp.20-27.

This paper describes the database design methodology used by
the Wholesale Data Administration function at Manufacturers
Hanover Trust Company, a large US support a large integrated
real-time application.

(Hoare, 1972) C.A.R. Hoare. Notes on data
structuring. In: Structured Programming, by O.-J.
Dahl, E.W. Dijkstra and C.A.R. Hoare. Academic
Press, London, England, 1972, pp.83-174.

his monograph is the foundation contribution of Professor
Hoare to the understanding of the design of data structures.

(Hotaka, 1982) R. Hotaka. The Design of an
Integrated Data Dictionary Directory System. In:
(Yao et al, 1982a), pp.56-70.

A practical way of implementation of Data Dictionary/Directory
(DD/D) Systems is not well established. A method using
self-descriptive DBMS is presented in this paper emphasising
the DD/D System implementation aspects.

(Hotaka, 1984) R. Hotaka. Statistical Database
Design Method. Res. Rep., Univ. of Tsukuba,
Japan, Jun 84, pp.8.

A statistical data model is presented. Using this data model
statistical DB design procedures are proposed to obtain
canonical representations of statistical traditional files.

(Hotaka and Tsubaki, 1981) R. Hotaka, M. Tsubaki.
Sentential Database Design Method. Discussion Paper
Ser. No.105 (81-6), Institute of Socio-Economic
Planning, Univ. of Tsukuba, Sakura, Japan, Feb 81,
pp.12.

The Sentential Database Design Method (SDDM) is presented in
this report. This method uses simple sentences to represent
information requirements. SDDM is based on its own data model
in which the notions of generalisation and specialisation are
incorporated.

(Housel et al, 1979) B.C. Housel, V. Waddle, S.B. Yao. The Functional Dependency Model for Logical Database Design. Proc. 5th Int. Conf. on VLDB, Rio de Janeiro, Brazil, Oct 79, pp.194-208.

A number of concepts to be used as a basis for a flexible and powerful conceptual database design tool and methodology are introduced in this paper.

(Hubbard, 1982) G.U. Hubbard. A Technique for Automated Logical Database Design. In: (Yao et al, 1982a), pp.219-227.

(Inmon, 1981) W.H. Inmon. Effective Data Base Design. Prentice-Hall, Englewood Cliffs, NY, 1981, pp.xi+228.

This book explains the entire process of the implementation of an effective application using a DBMS. The writing is simple and clear with a continuous series of examples.
Any potential user of a DBMS can read the book to have a complete idea of the process of developing an effective application.

(Irani et al, 1979) K.B. Irani, S. Purkayastha, T.J. Teorey. A Designer for DBMS-Processable Logical Database Structures. Proc. 5th Int. Conf. on VLDB, Rio de Janeiro, Brazil, Oct 79, pp.219-231.

This paper gives an overview of a partially automated design tool for producing database structures for the implementation design. The methodology applies to both the network and the hierarchical data models.

(ISO, 1981) ISO/TC97/SC5/WG3. Concepts and Terminology for the Conceptual Sohema. J.J. van Griethuysen et al (Eds). Preliminary Report for Review and Comment only, Feb 81.

(ISO, 1982) ISO/TC97/SC5/WG3. Concepts and Terminology for the Conceptual Schema and the Information Base. J.J. van Griethuysen (Ed). Mar 82.

These are the ISO/TC97/SC5/WG3 preliminary and the final reports on the concept schema and information base.
The final report explains the roles and concepts for a

conceptual schema providing a framework for discussion and for
the design of conceptual schema languages.

(Jajodia et al, 1983) S. Jajodia, P.A. Ng, F.N.
Springsteel. The Problem of Equivalence for
Entity-Relationship Diagrams. IEEE Trans. on
Software Engin., Vol.SE-9, No.5, Sept 83,
pp.617-630.

This paper investigates the equivalence of entity-relationship
diagrams, namely when two entity-relationship models should be
considered equivalent in the sense of representing the same
information about the real world.

(Jardine, 1977) D.A. Jardine (Ed). The ANSI/SPARC
DBMS Model. Noth-Holland, Amsterdam, The
Netherlands, 1977, pp.vii+225.

This volume contains the papers presented at the second SHARE
Working Conference held in Montreal in April 76. These papers
and the discussions on them are included in edited form;
these address many concepts contained in the 1975 ANSI/SPARC
DBMS Study Group report.

(Jarke and Koch, 1984) M. Jarke, J. Koch. Query
Optimization in Database Systems. Computing Surv.,
Vol.16, No.2, Jun 84, pp.111-152.

The goal of the paper is to review query optimisation
techniques in the common framework of relational calculus.
Section 4 of the paper is pertinent to physical DB design, in
fact it analyses the implementation of the operations that
return the data requested by a query.

(Kahn, 1976) B.K. Kahn. A Method for Describing
Information Required by the Database Design Process.
Proc. ACM-SIGMOD Int. Conf. on Management of
Data, Washington, D.C., Jun 76, pp.53-64.

The author believes that a framework for the collection,
expression, analysis and synthesis of information requirements
is the foundation of the database design process.
The author proposes a framework with these characteristics
which is based on the "information structure perspective" and
"usage perspective" and which provides a mechanism for these
activities.

(Kahn, 1982) B.K. Kahn. LDDM - A Structured Logical Database Design Methodology. In: (Yao et al, 1982a), pp.31-55.

(Kahn and Lumsden, 1983) B.K. Kahn, E.W. Lumsden. A User-Oriented Framework for Data Dictionary Systems. DATA BASE, Vol.15, No.1, Fall 83, pp.28-36.

This paper presents a new framework for analysing data dictionary systems that encompasses the most critical environmental dependencies and organisational requirements.

(Kalinichenko, 1976) L.A. Kalinichenko. Relational-Network Data Structure Mapping. In: (Nijssen, 1976a), pp.303-309.

A method of mapping from relational to network schema is proposed in this paper.

(Kambayashi et al, 1982) Y. Kambayashi, K. Tanaka, S. Yajima. Problems of Relational Database Design. In: (Yao et al, 1982a), pp.172-227.

(Katz, 1983) R.H. Katz. Managing the Chip Design Database. Computer, Vol.16, No.12, Dec 83, pp.26-36.

Design data management is introduced in this paper; it is a crucial feature of an integrated design system. In fact it bridges the gap between design tools and database systems, creating an integrated tool environment.

(Katz and Lehman, 1984) R.H. Katz, T.J. Lehman. Database Support for Versions and Alternatives of Large Design Files. IEEE Trans. on Software Engin., Vol.SE-10, No.2, Mar 84, pp.191-200.

Design versions and alternatives in an engineering database are identified together with the roles they play. The authors describe a storage structure for version management that combines aspects of differential files and shadows. Versions are encoded differentially while keeping the access overhead reasonable.

(Keller and Ullman, 1984) A.M. Keller, J.D. Ullman. On Complementary and Independent Mappings on Databases. In: Proc. ACM-SIGMOD Ann. Meeting. B. Yormark (Ed). Boston, MA, Jun 84, pp.143-148.

The relationship between independent and complementary mappings are formally addressed in this paper.

(Kent, 1976) W. Kent. New Criteria for the Conceptual Model. In: Systems for Large Data Bases. P.C. Lockemann and E.J. Neuhold (Eds). North-Holland, 1976, pp.1-11.

(Kent, 1977) W. Kent. Entities and Relationships in Information. In: (Nijssen, 1977a), pp.67-91.

This paper anticipates some of Bill Kent thoughts on the representation of information in computers that are presented in (Kent, 1978).

(Kent, 1978) W. Kent. Data and Reality. North-Holland, Amsterdam, the Netherlands, 1978, pp.xv+211.

In the final chapter of this book Bill Kent says: "This book projects a philosophy that life and reality are at bottom amorphous, disordered, contradictory, inconsistent, non-rational, and non-objective. Science and much of western philosophy have in the past presented us with the illusion that things are otherwise. Rational views of the universe are idealized models which only approximate reality. The approximations are useful. The models are successful often enough in predicting the behavior of things that they provide a useful foundation for science and technology. But they are ultimately only approximations of reality, and non-unique at that."
Some approximations of reality are the concern of the database designer.

(Kent, 1981a) W. Kent. Data Model Theory Meets a Practical Application. Proc. 7th Int. Conf. on VLDB, Cannes, France, Sept 81, pp.13-22.

The author reports on some insights gained while using an experimental data description tool based on entity/relationship concepts. For example, a binary-relation form of ERA model is considered to be very useful, but troublesome.

(Kent, 1981b) W. Kent. Consequences of Assuming a Universal Relation. ACM Trans. on DB Syst., Vol.6, No.4, Dec 81, pp.539-556.

The author attacks the problem of assuming a universal relation. And he shows that the decomposition approach to database design becomes virtually indistinguishable from the synthetic approach.

(Kerschberg et al, 1976) L. Kerschberg, A. Klug, D. Tsichritzis. A Taxonomy of Data Models. In: Systems for Large Data Bases. P.C. Lockemann and E.J. Neuhold (Eds), North-Holland, 1976, pp.43-64.

This paper classifies some conceptual data models within a taxonomy framework consisting of the following parameters: graph theoretic versus set theoretic models, mathematical foundations, terminology, and semantic levels of abstraction.

(Kershberg et al, 1980) L. Kerschberg, M. Brodie, P. Buneman, B. Housel, D. McLeod, G. Wiederhold. Information Modeling Tools for Database Design. Inform. Modeling Group Rep., Panel on Logical DB Design, DB Directions III, Fort Lauderdale, FL, Oct 80, pp.ii+26.

This report contains the results of the working group on information modeling. The three main issues addressed are: 1) the information modeling process, 2) the database workbench concept and 3) database communication.

(Klug, 1979) A. Klug. Entity-Relationship Views Over Uninterpreted Enterprise Schemas. Proc. Int. Conf. on E/R Approach to Syst. Analysis and Design, Dec 79, Los Angeles, CA, pp.52-72.

The author believes that the way to provide multiple enterprise level interfaces is to have an underlying uninterpreted conceptual schema and a number of translators to present this schema in terms of entities and relationships or in other formats. Some basic constructs and an algorithm for traslating them are given in the paper.

(Leavenworth, 1981) B. Leavenworth. Database Views Using Data Abstraction. IBM Res. Rep. RC8722, IBM T.J. Watson Res. Center, Yorktown Heights, NY, Feb 81, pp.20.

his report describes the use of a module interconnection anguage to define a DB schema, in conjunction with the use of ata abstractions to define entity types and relationships. he experimental programming system which supports data bstractions and which has been developed is called ADAPT ystem.

data abstraction called a "form" is introduced; this data bstraction allows different views of the hierarchical model nd transformations between that model and the relational odel. The form abstraction is resulted as a convenient ehicle for defining different user views and a communication ool between different data models.

(Leonard and Luong, 1981) M. Leonard, B.T. Luong. Information Systems Design Approach Integrating Data and Transactions. Proc. 7th Int. Conf. on VLDB, Cannes, France, Sept 81, pp.235-246.

his approach is part of a general framework of information ystem design and its aim is to clarify the interdependence etween data and transactions; it is based on the relational ata model for the data representation and on Petri model for he representation of transactions.

(Leong-Hong and Plagman, 1982) B.W. Leong-Hong, B.K. Plagman. Data Dictionary/Directory Systems. Administration, Implementation and Usage. Wiley, New York, NY, 1982, pp.xviii+328.

he dictionary and directory technology is fully presented in his book. The book comprehensively describes a DD/DS from everal perspectives: functional use, design, implementation, nd administration.

(Lindencrona-Ohlin, 1979) E. Lindencrona-Ohlin. A Study on Conceptual Data Modeling. Ph.D. Dissertation, Chalmers Univ. of Technology, Dept. of Computer Sciences, Gothenburg, Sweden, 79, pp.151+appendix.

his study concentrates on informal definitions of the ontents of conceptual level design and it identifies problem reas.

Further, an attempt is made to identify and discuss semantical
aspects of conceptual database design. For this purpose a
number of design methods are analysed.

(Loomis et al, 1981) M.E.S. Loomis, M.V. Mannino
F.W. Allen. Fundamentals of Integrated
Dictionary/Directory Systems. Inform. and
Management, Vol.4, 1981, pp.287-295.

Integrated Data Dictionary Systems (DDS) have important role
in controlling both centralised and distributed information
resources; these roles are investigated in this paper.

(Lum et al, 1979) V. Lum, S. Ghosh, M
Schkolnick, D. Jefferson, S. Su, J. Fry, T
Teorey, B. Yao. 1978 New Orleans Data Base Desig
Workshop Report. IBM Res. Rep. RJ 2554, IBM Res
Lab., San Jose, CA, Jul 79, pp.117.

In October 1978 some of the leading experts on database desig:
from around the world assembled in New Orleans to discuss
evaluate and set directions for research, development an
practice of database design. This report summarises thei
thinking.

(Lum et al, 1984) V. Lum, P. Dadam, R. Erbe, J
Guenauer, P. Pistor, G. Walch, H. Werner, J
Woodfill. Designining DBMS Support for the Tempora
Dimension. In: Proc. ACM-SIGMOD Ann. Meeting
B. Yormark (Ed). Boston, MA, Jun 84, pp.115-130.

The need to have history data support in DBMS is discussed i
this paper. The authors feel that it is necessary to suppor
historical data access paths in particular for specifi
applications such as law and office applications. A possibl
design is proposed.

(McCracken and Jackson, 1982) D.D. McCracken, M.A
Jackson. Life Cycle Concept Considered Harmful
SOFTWARE ENGIN. NOTES, Vol.7, No.2, Apr 82
pp.29-32.

The authors believe that the "life cycle concept" is unsuite
to the needs of the 1980's in developing systems. The
present three groups of criticism for the life cycle concep
and they sketch two scenarios of system development processe
that they believe to be impossible to force into the lif

cycle concept without torturing either logic or language or both. The two scenarios are: prototyping and a process of system development done by the end-user and an analyst in this sequence: implement, design, specify, redesign, re-implement.

(Machgeels, 1976) C. Machgeels. A Procedural Language for Expressing Integrity Constraints in the Coexistence Model. In: (Nijssen, 1976a), pp.293-301.

A procedural language, PLIC, is defined in this paper. It allows to express integrity constraints at the conceptual schema level.

(Macdonald and Palmer, 1982) I.G. Macdonald, I.R. Palmer. System Development in a Shared Data Environment. In: (Olle et al, 1982), pp.235-283.

This paper describes the D2S2 (Development of Data Sharing Systems) methodology. This is a pragmatic methodology for the analysis and development of systems. It has been used in Europe for more than a decade in different systems environments, particularly in areas where data sharing is required and where database solutions are appropriate.
This paper explains the methodology and shows how it would be used particularly during the analysis stage.

(Maddison et al, 1982) R.N. Maddison, G.J. Baker, L. Bhabuta, G. Fitzgerald, K. Hidle, J.H.T. Song, N. Stokes, J.R.G. Wood. Feature Analysis of Contemporary Information System Methodologies: A Collective View. 1982, pp.49.

The authors identify a framework to evaluate seven methodologies. These methodologies are: ACM/PCM, D2S2, ISAC, LBMS-SDM, NIAM, SASD and SYSDOC.

(Maggiolini, 1981) P. Maggiolini. Costi e benefici di un sistema informativo. Etas Libri, Sonzogno (MI), Italy, 1981, pp.252.

The main theme of the book is the cost/benefit analysis of information systems. The initial chapters are on information systems in general and pertinent to this bibliography.

(Malhotra et al, 1981) A. Malhotra, H.M.
Markowitz, D.P. Pazel. The EAS-E Programming
Language. IBM Res. Rep. RC8935, IBM T.J. Watson
Res. Center, Yorktown Heights, NY, Jul 81, pp.246.

(March, 1983) S.T. March. Techniques for
Structuring Database Records. Computing Surv.,
Vol.15, No.1, Mar 83, pp.45-79.

An important issue in database design is how to physically
organise the data in secondary memory so that the information
requirements of the user community can be met efficiently.
The author identifies by "record structures" of a database
this physical organisation.
This paper presents alternative techniques that can be used to
quickly determine efficient record structures for large shared
databases.

(March and Severance, 1978) S.T. March, D.G.
Severance. A Mathematical Modeling Approach to the
Automatic Selection of Database Designs. Proc.
ACM-SIGMOD 6th Int. Conf. on Management of Data,
1978, pp.52-65.

A specific research effort conducted by the Management
Information Systems Research Center at the University of
Minnesota has developed a design system aimed at helping a
systems analyst design a physical database. This paper
presents an overview of that system and provides an index to
additional, more detailed documentation.

(Markowitz et al, 1981) H.M. Markowitz, A.
Malhotra, D.P. Pazel. The ER and EAS Formalism for
System Modeling, and the EAS-E Language. IBM Res.
Rep. RC8802, IBM T.J. Watson Res. Center,
Yorktown Heights, NY, Apr 81, pp.20.

(Matsuka et al, 1982) H. Matsuka, S. Uno, M.
Sibuya. Specific Requirements in Engineering Data
Base. In: (Yao and Kunii, 1982), pp.345-356.

(Meltzer, 1976) H.S. Meltzer. Structure and
Redundancy in the Conceptual Schema in the
Administration of Very Large Data Base. In:
Systems for Large Data Bases. P.C. Lockemann and
E.J. Neuhold (Eds). North-Holland, 1976, pp.13-25.

(Meyer   and   Schneider,   1979)   B.E.   Meyer,   H.-J.
Schneider.   Tools for Information System Design and
Realization.   In: Formal Models and Practical Tools
for Information System Design.   H.-J. -Schneider
(Ed),   Noth-Holland,   Amsterdam,   the   Netherlands,
1979, pp.1-29.

This paper introduces two new concepts: a method and a model
base system which constitute a system that enables the casual
user in a multiuser environment to solve his problems easily
and fast with a minimum of programming efforts and a maximum
of system support.   The authors have developed a system
monitor,   called   BOSS,   which performs and controls the
communication between model, method and DB system on the one
hand and the user on the other.

(Mijares et al, 1976) I. Mijares, R.   Peebles.   A
Methodology for the Design of Logical Data Base
Structures. In: (Nijssen, 1976a), pp.25-47.

This paper presents a methodology to create the database
logical structure from information given by the user.

(Mohan and Popescu-Zeletin, 1982) C.   Mohan, R.
Popescu-Zeletin.   Impact of Distributed Data Base
Management on the ISO-OSI and ANSI/SPARC Frameworks.
Proc.   15th Hawaii Int. Conf. on Syst. Sciences,
Honolulu, Hawaii, Jan 82, pp.532-542.

The authors present the key features of a logical architecture
that they support for DDBMS.   This architecture takes into
account the ANSI/SPARC framework and the ISO/OSI reference
model.

(Molina, 1979) F.W. Molina. A Practical Data Base
Design Method.   DATA BASE, Vol.11, No.1, Summer 79,
pp.3-11.

The method suggested in this paper is based on a particular
perception of what a database should be.   To make this
perception valid, the context in which the total information
activity takes place is examined first. This permits focusing
attention on the environment in which databases normally
exist, providing a conceptual background for the proposed
design approach.

(Motro, 1984) A. Motro. Browsing in Loosely Structured Database. In: Proc. ACM-SIGMOD Ann. Meeting. B. Yormark (Ed). Boston, MA, Jun 84, pp.197-207.

A database architecture that deemphasizes structure is introduced in this paper. The database is only a loosely structured DB, that is heaps of facts instead of highly structured data. This architecture avoids the traditional dichotomy between "schema" and "data", and it incorporates a single mechanism for defining both inference rules and integrity constraints.

(Moulin et al, 1976) P. Moulin, J. Randon, S. Savoysky, S. Spaccapietra, H. Tardieu, M. Teboul. Conceptual Model as a Data Base Design Tool. In: (Nijssen, 1976a), pp.221-238.

The conceptual modelling subject is investigated in this paper. It is one of the first papers which makes clear that the conceptual model must not be influenced by the present DBMS implementation capabilities.

(Mumford, 1984) E. Mumford. Participative Systems Design. The Computer Jour., Short Note, Vol.27, No.3, Aug 84, p.283.

The author relates this short note to the paper by Wood-Harper and Fitzgerald, (Wood-Harper and Fitzgerald, 1982), and the subsequent note by Cookson, (Cookson, 1983), on different approaches to systems analysis.
The author is not in accord with the belief of the cited authors that participative design is concerned primarily or only with implementation. Consequently she shows as the participative systems design process covers the traditional systems design model of investigation, analysis, design and implementation.

(Navathe, 1980) S.B. Navathe. Schema Analysis for Database Restructuring. ACM Trans. on DB Syst., Vol.5, No.2, Jun 80, pp.157-184.

The distinction between hierarchical and nonhierarchical data relationships is discussed in this paper, and a classification for database schemata is proposed. Application of the schema analysis methodology to restructuring specification is also discussed.

(Navathe and Fry, 1976) S.B.   Navathe,   J.P.   Fry.
Restructuring for Large Databases: Three Levels of
Abstraction. ACM Trans. on DB Syst., Vol.1,   No.2,
Jun 76, pp.138-158.

restructuring function needs restructuring operations and
he implementation of these operations in a software system.
his paper addresses the restructuring operations problem
efining the semantics of the restructuring of tree structured
atabases.

(Navathe   and   Gadgil,   1982)   S.B.   Navathe,   S.G.
Gadgil.   A Methodology for View Integration in
Logical Database Design. Proc. 8th Int. Conf. on
VLDB, Mexico City, Mexico, Sept 82, pp.142-164.

(Navathe and Schkolnick, 1978) S.B.   Navathe,   M.
Schkolnick. View Representation in Logical Database
Design.   Proc.   ACM-SIGMOD   Int.   Conf.   on
Management of Data, Austin, TX, Jun 78, pp.144-156.

his paper proposes a scheme for view representation which
acilitates the process of view integration. The problem of
iew integration is partly addressed.

(Nijssen, 1976a) G.M. Nijssen (Ed).   Modelling in
Data Base Management Systems. North-Holland,
Amsterdam, The Netherlands, 1976, pp.vii+418.

hese are the proceedings of the IFIP Working Conference on
odelling in Data Base Management Systems held in
reudenstadt, Germany, Jan 76.
he majority of the papers is concentrated on conceptual
odelling, then the pertinent papers are individually
eferenced by the name of the first author.

(Nijssen,   1976b)   G.M.   Nijssen.   A   Gross
Architecture for the Next Generation Database
Management. In: (Nijssen, 1976a), pp.1-24.

his paper forecasts in 1976 the architecture of present DBMS,
d it is still infuential for the database design practice.

(Nijssen, 1977a) G.M. Nijssen (Ed). Architecture
and Models in Data Base Management Systems.
North-Holland, Amsterdam, The Netherlands, 1977,
pp.viii+326.

These are the proceedings of the IFIP Working Conference or
Database Management that was held in Nice, France, in January
1977. The concepts for the conceptual schema were the mair
topics for the conference. Many papers are relevant to this
bibliography and they are individually referenced.

(Nijssen, 1977b) G.M. Nijssen. Current Issues in
Conceptual Schema Concepts. In: (Nijssen, 1977a)
pp.31-65.

This paper presents the synthesis of papers presented at th
1976 IFIP TC2 Conference and of additional research effor
performed by the author during 1976.

(Nijssen, 1978) G.M. Nijssen. An Overall Model fo
Information Systems Design and Associated Practica
Tools. CINECA Rep., Casalecchio di Reno (BO)
Italy, Oct 78, pp.191.

This report contains two papers, the first, as in the title
describes an approach to information systems development. Th
second paper, entitled "A conceptual framework for informatio
analysis", is on the conceptual schema concept.

(Oftedal and Solvberg, 1981) H. Oftedal, A
Solvberg. Data Base Design Constrained by Traffi
Load Estimates. Inform. Syst., Vol.6, No.4, 81
pp.267-282.

A method for including traffic load estimates in early desig
components is proposed in this paper. This method can be use
for developing a user interactive specification tool.

(Olle, 1978) T.W. Olle. Multistage Data Definitic
in a Multicomponent DBMS Architecture. Ir
Databases: Improving Usability and Responsiveness
B. Shneiderman (Ed), Academic Press, New York, N\
1978, pp.343-370.

(Olle, 1983) T.W. Olle. Information systems design - where do we stand? _Inform._ _Tech._ _Training_, Vol.1, No.2, May 83, pp.88-91.

This article takes a broad look at the topic of information systems design with special reference to the activities of IFIP Working Group 8.1 (Design and Evaluation of Information Systems). This group has initiated a three-stage exercise entitled a Comparative Review of Information Systems Design Methodologies (often identified by the acronym CRIS). See reference (Olle et al, 1982) for the proceedings of the first CRIS conference held in May 82 and (Olle et al, 1983) for the proceedings of the second CRIS conference held in July 83.

(Olle et al, 1982) T.W. Olle, H.G. Sol, A.A. Verrijn-Stuart (Eds). _Information_ _Systems_ _Design_ _Methodologies:_ _A_ _Comparative_ _Review._ North-Holland, Amsterdam, The Netherlands, 1982, pp.x+648.

These are the proceedings of the IFIP WG8.1 Working Conference on Comparative Review of Information Systems Design Methodologies (CRIS). The conference has been held at Noordwijkerhout, The Netherlands in May 1982.
This book represents an attempt to review and compare different information systems (IS) methodologies. But it is more successful in reviewing methodologies for the design of IS subsystems. In fact it contains several papers on methodologies for data analysis; some specific methods for handling particular problems of information systems design; but it does not contain a single complete information system design methodology as the title promises.

(Olle et al, 1983) T.W. Olle, H.G. Sol, C.J. Tully (Eds). _Information_ _Systems_ _Design_ _Methodologies:_ _a_ _Feature_ _Analysis._ Partecipants edition. North-Holland, Amsterdam, The Netherlands, 1983, pp.ix+226.

These are the proceedings of the second CRIS working conference held in July 83. They consist of a number of feature analysis of the methodologies included in the first proceedings (Olle et al, 1982).

(Ong et al, 1984) J. Ong, D. Fogg, M. Stonebraker. Implemetation of Data Abstraction in the Relational Database System INGRES. _SIGMOD_ _RECORD_, Vol.14, No.1, Mar 84, pp.1-14.

This paper presents the design and implementation of an "abstract data type (ADT) facility" which has been added to the INGRES database manager.
This implementation of ADTs allows a user to register ADTs and ADT operators with the run-time database manager, declare column values of relations to be instances of ADTs, and formulate queries containing references to ADTs and ADT operators.

(Oren and Aschim, 1979) O. Oren, F. Aschim. Statistics for the Usage of a Conceptual Data Model as a Basis for Logical Data Base Design. Proc. 5th Int. Conf. on VLDB, Rio de Janeiro, Brazil, Oct 79, pp.140-145.

The database design aid, SYDADA, is introduced in this paper. The requirements specification expressed in the language SYSDOC is the input to SYDADA. A result of the analysis of requirements, implemented through SYDADA, is a set of statistics showing how the various parts of the data are forecast to be used; these statistics can be used as a basis for conceptual database design.

(OSI, 1981) ISO/TC97/SC16. Data Processing - Open Systems Interconnection - Basic Reference Model. Computer Networks, Vol.5, No.2, Apr 81, pp.81-118.

(OSI, 1982) ISO/TC97. Information processing systems - Open systems interconnection - Basic reference model. Draft Int. Standard ISO/DIS 7498, Int. Organization for Standardization, Apr 82, pp.78.

The seven layers basic reference model for open systems interconnection is presented in these two references. This model is influential especially for the design of distributed databases.
Other pertinent references on ISO/OSI are (desJardins, 1981), (Mohan and Popescu-Zeletin, 1982), (Popescu-Zeletin and Weber, 1980) and (Steel, 1982).

(Palmer, 1978) I.R. Palmer. Practicalities in Applying a Formal Methodology to Data Analysis. Proc. NYU Symp. on DB Design, May 78, pp.67-84. (also in (Yao et al, 1982a), pp.147-171.)

(Paolini and Pelagatti, 1977) P. Paolini, G. Pelagatti. Formal Definition of Mappings in a Data Base. Proc. ACM-SIGMOD Int. Conf. on Management of Data, Toronto, Canada, Aug 77, pp.40-46.

he problem of mapping between different levels of a database s studied in this paper. A method for formally defining the apping between external and conceptual databases is proposed.

(Parent, 1981) C. Parent. Projet SCOOP - Etude des modeles semantiques de donnees. Rapport RT.SCOOP 81.5, Systemes Informatique, Institut de Programmation, Universite P. et M. Curie, Paris, France, May 81, pp.31.

his report surveys the semantic data models as candidate odels for the conceptual schema of a DDBMS with heterogeneous xternal schemas. The main characteristics a semantic data odel has to have to be used in this contex are identified.

(Parimala et al, 1984) N. Parimala, N. Prakash, N. Bolloju. New Corecs and New Cosets in Admin. The Computer Jour., Vol.27, No.4, Nov 84, pp.310-314.

dmin is a DBMS based on the network data model. In Admin the ecord type is referred to as corec type and the set type as oset type. The authors illustrate the way in which corec ypes and coset types can be constructed using other corec and oset types. Then it is shows a way of defining new types in network data model.
ee (Prakash et al, 1984) for aspects of specifying integrity onstraints in Admin.

(Philips and Jackson, 1984) R. Philips, M.S. Jackson. Data access and storage in an entity relationship database system. Interfaces in Computing, Vol.2, No.1, Feb 84, pp.31-43.

is paper describes the choices of the designers of a DBMS thin a database project at Manchester University (UK). e paper discusses the criteria for the choice of the entity altionship model to be used for the implementation component the DB design process. The structure of the data storage bsystem is described and two data storage models are scussed.

(Popescu-Zeletin   and   Weber,   1980)   R
Popescu-Zeletin, H. Weber. Some consideration.
about distributed data bases on public networks
In: Distributed Data Bases. C. Delobel and W
Litwin (Eds), North-Holland, 1980, pp.1-15.

This paper analyses the services proposed in the ISO model fo
Open Systems Interconnection (OSI) with respect to their us
as a basis for the development of a DDBMS on public networks.
The authors identify some parameters of DDB systems whos
value may have impact on the feasibility of such a system on
public network.
The ESA (Evolutionary System Architecture) architecture for
DDBMS on a public network is proposed.

(Prakash et al, 1984) N. Prakash, N. Parimala, N
Bolloju. Specifying Integrity Constraints in
Network DBMS. The Computer Jour., Vol.27, No.3, Au
84, pp.209-217.

The problem of specifying integrity constraints in a networ
DBMS is addressed in this paper. The authors consider th
integrity constraint facilities offered by the Admin DBMS. I
Admin it is possible to define multiple levels of subschema c
a given schema. An implementation mechanism is reported i
the paper and it has been successfully implemented by th
authors.
See (Parimala et al, 1984) for other details on the Admi
DBMS.

(Prowse and Johnson, 1980) P.H.   Prowse,   R.(
Johnson.   A natural language data base interface t
the user. The Computer Jour., Vol.23, No.1, 198:
pp.22-25.

The authors introduce two techniques that allow the user t
understand more fully the implications of a design. Fewe
changes are forecast to be neccosary later due to errors :
the design, with a resulting decline in development times a
costs for new projects.

(Raver and Hubbard, 1977) N. Raver, G.U. Hubbar
Automated logical data base design: Concepts a
applications. IBM Syst. Jour., Vol.16, No.3, 197
pp.287-312.

This paper describes the design effort for an integrated da
base and then develops techniques for automating significa

parts of it.

(Reuter and Kinzinger, 1984) A. Reuter, H. Kinzinger. Automatic Design of the Internal Schema for a CODASYL Database System. IEEE Trans. on Software Engin., Vol.SE-10, No.4, Jul 84, pp.358-375.

A tool for designing an "optimal" physical database is described in this paper. The tool has been developed for the DBMS UDS that is a CODASYL-like. The paper describes its basic functions, the results of validation experiments of this design aid, named DAIS.

(Ries, 1982) D.R. Ries (Ed). An Architectural Framework for Database Standardization (Draft). The Database Architectural Framework Task Group, Jul 82, pp.33.

This report describes a database architectural framework for integrating distributed databases, multiple data models, and data dictionaries. The framework supports the concept of families of database standards.

(Rolin, 1980) P. Rolin. Using Petri-Nets in Measurement of a Distributed Data Base System. SIRIUS Rep. MES-I-002, INRIA, Le Chesnay, France, Mar 80, pp.14.

(Rolland, 1983) C. Rolland. Database Dynamics. DATA BASE, Vol.14, No.3, Spring 83, pp.32-43.

This paper argues for a global description, at a conceptual level, of the structure and the behaviour of data, and an automatic control of the flow of data in the course of time.

(Rolland and Richard, 1980) C. Rolland, C. Richard. A Conceptual Approach for the Design and Evolution Control of Distributed Data Systems. Rep. SIRIUS MOD-I-032, CNRS Lab. of Nancy, France, Apr 80, pp.49.

(Rothnie and Hardgrave, 1976) J.B.   Rothnie, W.T. Hardgrave.   Data Model Theory: A Beginning. Proc. 5th Texas Conf. on Computing Syst., Oct 76.

The need for a general framework for data model definition is discussed in this paper and an initial framework is defined.

(Roussopoulos, 1982) N. Roussopoulos. The Logical Access Path Schema of a Database. IEEE Trans. on Software Engin., Vol.SE-8, No.6, Nov 82, pp.563-573.

The author introduces in this paper a new schema of a database in order to model the accessing requirements, because he believes that both the design and the maintenance of any database requires such a model.

(Ruchti, 1976) J. Ruchti. Data Descriptions Embedded in Context. In: (Nijssen, 1976a), pp.111-123.

The notion of "conceptual language" as the means to write the conceptual schema is introduced in this paper. Most important features of such a language are dealt in the paper.

(Sakai, 1979) H. Sakai. A unified approach to the logical design of a hierarchical data model. Proc. Int. Conf. on E/R Approach to Syst. Analysis and Design, Dec 79, Los Angeles, CA, pp.73-86.

The Entity-Relationship model is used to describe the conceptual schema, and a translation process from the E/R model to the hierarchical model is proposed.

(Sakai, 1981) H. Sakai. A Method for Defining Information Structures and Transactions in Conceptual Schema Design. Proc. 7th Conf. on VLDB, Cannes, France, Sept 81, pp.225-234.

A method for defining the conceptual schema is discussed within the framework of the Entity-Relationship model.

(Sarda and Isaac, 1981) N.L. Sarda, J.R. Isaac. Computer Aided Design of Database Internal Schema. Int. Jour. of Computer and Inform. Sciences, Vol.10, No.4, 1981, pp.219-234.

This paper introduces a three step approach to the design of internal schema. Instead of attempting to formulate a single optimisation model, this paper suggests a step by step solution where each step is supported by an automatic tool. These tools are some of the aids provided by the Computer Aided Design system for design of Information Systems (CADIS).

(Schiel, 1982) U. Schiel. A Semantic Data Model and its Mapping to an Internal Relational Model. CREST Course: Database - Role and Structures. Univ. of East Anglia, Norwich, England, Sept 82, pp.28. (also in (Stocker et al, 1984).)

The first part of the paper presents a semantic data model called Temporal-Hierarchic Model (THM). This model offers a graphical framework for illustrating a conceptual schema and a conceptual schema language.
The second part of the paper shows the mapping between the conceptual schema in THM and the implementation schema in relational model.

(Schkolnick, 1978) M. Schkolnick. A Survey of Physical Database Design Methodology and Techniques. IBM Res. Rep. RJ 2306, IBM Res. Lab. San Jose, CA, Aug 78, pp.14. (also in Proc. 4th Int. Conf. on VLDB, West-Berlin, Germany, Sept 1978, pp.474-487.)

The problem of physical database design has received considerable attention. This paper provides a survey of a large number of design techniques that have resulted from this activity.
Specifically, the author reviews literature which addresses the file structuring problem, the access path selection problem, the record segmentation and allocation problem, and the reorganization problem. Buffer management, memory hierarchies, and file allocation, which also affect the performance of batabases are not considered. But complementaty survey are suggested to the interested reader.
It is also reported the hierarchical breakdown of the DB design problem that was proposed at a seminar on DB design at IBM Research Laboratory, San Jose, in late 1976.

(Schkolnick, 1982) M. Schkolnick. Physical Database Design Techniques. In: (Yao and Kunii, 1982), pp.229-252.

(Schmid, 1977) H.A. Schmid. An Analysis of Some
Constructs for Conceptual Models. In: (Nijssen,
1977a), pp.119-148.

The author analyses some of the problems which arise in the
selection of a model for the conceptual schema.
At the beginning of the paper he introduces an abstraction
process scheme that usefully clarifies the different levels of
conceptual models. And, with this reference in mind, the
author says that a conceptual schema should be described
rather in terms of the 'conceptual information structure
level' than of the 'conceptual data level'.
Some constructs are defined for the conceptual schema. To
compare different constructs he uses mappings that define
between the constructs. Static and also dynamic aspects of
modelling are considered.

(Schreiber and Martella, 1979) F.A. Schreiber, G.
Martella. Creating a Conceptual Model of a Data
Dictionary for Distributed Data Bases. DATA BASE,
Vol.11, No.1, Summer 79, pp.12-18.

An integrated tool, called Distributed System Dictionary, is
proposed in this paper for the design and the management of a
distributed database.

(SECT/IEEE, 1982) Software Engineering Technical
Committeee (SETC) of the IEEE Computer Society. A
Glossary of Software Engineering Terminology (IEEE
Project 729). Jul 82, pp.41.

This glossary was prepared by the Terminology Task Group of
the Software Engineering Standards Subcommittee of the SECT of
the IEEE Computer Society. The purpose of the glossary is to
identify terms currently used in software engineering and to
present the current meanings of these terms. It is intended
to serve as a useful reference for software engineers and for
those in related fields (one of these related fields is the
database area, and in particular the database design area),
and to promote clarity and consistency in the vocabulary of
software engineering.

(Sen, 1982) A. Sen. Logical Data Base Design: a
Management-Oriented Approach. Inform. and
Management, Vol.5, 1982, pp.77-85.

The author believes that it is very important to involve the
managers of the enterprise in the initial phase of the

conceptual design. So called 'surface semantic models' are used in this component to increase the managers' involvement. This paper proposes a special type of semantic model, a "hierarchical external view model", that has been successfully used to develop a database.

(Severance and Carlis, 1977) D.G. Severance, J.V. Carlis. A Practical Approach to Selecting Record Access Paths. Computing Surv., Vol.9, No.4, Dec 77, pp.259-272.

The purpose of this paper is to construct a concise framework for physical database design. Then it can be used as a concise index for the practitioner.
Three classes of data retrieval problems are identified, and alternative file structures and record search algorithms for these problems are analysed and compared. Then a method for constructing reasonable database organisations is introduced.

(Shave, 1981) M.J.R. Shave. Entities, Functions and Binary Relations: Steps to a Conceptual Schema. The Computer Jour., Vol.24, No.1, 1981, pp.42-47.

A DBMS-independent method of data analysis is decribed and assessed in relation to some more formal appoaches to data modelling.

(Shepherd and Kerschberg, 1984) A. Shepherd, L. Kerschberg. PRISM: A Knowledge Based System for Semantic Integrity Specification and Enforcement in Database Systems. In: Proc. ACM-SIGMOD Ann. Meeting. B. Yormark (Ed). Boston, MA, Jun 84, pp.307-315.

This paper presents a knowledge-based approach to the specification, design, implementation, and evolution of DB applications.
The semantic architecture of the PRISM system is described, together with the syntax and semantics of the constraint language.
User access to and control of matadata implies that user views of the knowledge base could be used to specify methodologies for DB design and to control access to DB applications.

(Shipman, 1981) D.W. Shipman. The Functional Data
Model and the Data Language DAPLEX. ACM Trans. on
DB Syst., Vol.6, No.1, Mar 81, pp.140-173.

This paper presents and motivates the DAPLEX language and the
underlying data model on which it is based.
DAPLEX is a data definition and manipulation language for
database systems, grounded in a concept of data representation
called the functional data model.

(Shmueli and Itai, 1984) O. Shmueli, A. Itai.
Maintenance of Views. In: Proc. ACM-SIGMOD Ann.
Meeting. B. Yormark (Ed). Boston, MA, Jun 84,
pp.240-255.

The dynamic maintenance of a class of views is examined in
this paper. It is proposed a maintenance mechanism for views
in that class. The authors show that the complexity of
updates is polynomial.
The paper suggests additional problems such as that of
maintaining multiple views, and that of extending the
mechanism to an off-line sequence of updates to base
relations.

(Shneiderman and Thomas, 1982) B. Shneiderman, G.
Thomas. An Architecture for Automatic Relational
Database System Conversion. ACM Trans. on DB
Syst., Vol.7, No.2, Jun 82, pp.235-257.

This paper addresses the problem of database conversion. A
set of 15 transformations for the relational model is
introduced and described in this paper.

(Shu et al, 1980) N.C. Shu, H.K.T. Wong, V.Y.
Lum. Forms Approach to Application Specification
for Database Design, IBM Res. Rep. RJ2687, IBM
Res. Lab. San Jose, CA, Feb 80, pp.46.

(Smith and Smith, 1977a) J.M. Smith, D.C.P. Smith.
Database Abstractions: Aggregation. Comm. of the
ACM, Vol.20, No.6, Jun 77, pp.405-413.

Aggregation is introduced as an abstraction which is important
in conceptualising the real world. Aggregation transforms a
relationship between objects into a higher level object.

(Smith and Smith, 1977b) J.M. Smith, D.C.P. Smith.
Database   Abstractions: Aggregation   and
Generalization. <u>ACM</u> <u>Trans.</u>   on <u>DB</u> <u>Syst.</u>, Vol.2,
No.2, Jun 77, pp.105-133.

Generalization is introduced as an abstraction which is
important in database design.   Generalization is an
abstraction which turns a class of objects into a generic
object.

(Smith and Smith, 1982) J.M. Smith, D.C.P.   Smith.
Principles of Database Conceptual Design. In: (Yao
et al, 1982a), pp.114-146.

Criteria and methodologies for the conceptual design of
databases,   particularly   in   large   and   sophisticated
applications, are addressed. This paper represents a further
step   forward   in database abstractions, following their
important papers (Smith and Smith, 1977a) and (Smith and
Smith, 1977b).

(Sockut and Goldberg, 1979) G.H. Sockut, R.P.
Goldberg.   Database Reorganization - Principles and
Practice. <u>Computing</u> <u>Surv.</u>, Vol.11, No.4, Vol.11,
No.4, Dec 79, pp.371-395.

The authors define "database reorganisation" as changing some
aspects of the way in which a database is arranged logically
and/or physically. Then reorganisation is a function that
must be supported by a database system. The paper introduces
the basic concepts of reorganisation.

(Solvberg, 1979) A. Solvberg. Software Requirement
Definition and Data Base Models. <u>Proc.</u> <u>5th</u> <u>Int.</u>
<u>Conf.</u> <u>on</u> <u>VLDB</u>, Rio de Janeiro, Brazil, Oct 79,
pp.111-118.

The author of this paper believes that the conceptual schema
should contain an "ontological" subschema, i.e. a model of
the reality of the application.
The ability to prove the semantical equivalence of databases
is a prerequisite to formal database design and database
integration. The paper shows that an ontological schema might
provide a basis for formal comparisons of the semantics of
different databases.

(Somogyi, 1981)   E.   Somogyi.   <u>System Development</u> <u>Methods</u>.   Butler   Cox   and   Partners   Ltd.,   London, England, Report Series No.25, Nov 81, pp.66.

Different system development approaches are identified and discussed in this report. The approaches are classified into those that concentrate on the development of the technological system itself, and those that concentrate on the planning process that should precede the introduction of a technological system.

(Spiegler, 1983) I. Spiegler.   Automatic Database Construction.   <u>DATA BASE</u>, Vol.14, No.3, Spring 83, pp.21-29.

A methodology for automating the construction of a database is described in this paper. The methodology makes use of three different tools that are integrated: 1)PSL/PSA as a front-end technique for stating system requirements; 2) a relational processor that transforms the requirements into Data Definition Language (DDL) statements of the ADABAS DBMS; 3) the DDL makes it possible to load and process data using standard routines available in the DBMS package.

(Stamper, 1977) R. Stamper. Physical Objects, Human Discourse and Formal Systems. In: (Nijssen, 1977a), pp.293-311.

This paper is about the LEGOL semantic model which treats the concepts of entity and identification from a point of view of systems analysis. This leads to a conceptual schema more complex than envisaged in previous discussions on DBMS.

(Steel, 1975) T.B. Steel. Data base standardization: a status report. In: <u>Database</u> <u>Description</u>. B.C.M. Douque and G.M. Nijssen (Eds), North-Holland, Amsterdam, the Netherlands, 1975, pp.183-198.

This paper is a report on the status of ANSI/X3/SPARC Study Group on DBMS. But in the latter portion of the paper the author introduces his personal view of the appropriate structure of a conceptual schema.

(Steel,   1982)   T.B.   Steel.   International
Standardization   and Distributed Data Bases. Proc.
2nd Int. Symp. on DDB, West Berlin, Germany, Sept
82, pp.1-7.

At the time of publication of this paper no active work on
standardisation relative to DDB is under way in the ISO. The
author believes that it will be several years before any
substantial change in this situation will obtain. But several
contemporary ISO efforts are laying the groundwork   for
eventual distributed database standards. Therefore the author
explores these efforts and attempts a prediction on the nature
of their development.

(Stocker, 1977) P.M. Stocker. The Structuring of
Data   Bases   at the Implementation Level.   In:
(Nijssen, 1977a), pp.261-276.

This paper is concerned with the physical design of a
database.   In particular it is concerned with structures,
access paths and logical layout on physical devices.

(Stocker et al, 1984) P.M. Stocker, P.M.D.   Gray,
M.P.   Atkinson   (Eds).   Databases - Role and
Structure. Cambridge Univ. Press, Cambridge, UK,
1984, pp.40.

This book contains the lecture notes of an advanced course of
the same name held at the University of East Anglia in
September 1982, sponsored by the Informatics Training Group of
the EEC Scientific and Technical Research Council and the
United Kingdom Science and Engineering Research Council.
The book presents an up-to-date report on current practice in
using and building databases.   Some papers cover different
aspects of DB design and are pertinent to this bibliography.
In particular they cover the data models topic (relational,
CODASYL, functional and semantic data models).

(Su and Lin, 1977) S.Y.W.   Su, B.J.   Lin.   A
Methodology of Application Program Analysis and
Conversion Based on Database Semantics.   Proc.
ACM-SIGMOD Int. Conf. on Management of Data,
Toronto, Canada, Aug 83, pp.75-87.

The problem of systematic conversion of application programs
due to database growth and modification is the concern of the
research reported in this paper.

(Sundgren, 1975) B. Sundgren. Theory of Data Bases. Petrocelli/ Charter, Ney York, NY, 1975, pp.xi+244.

This book reports parts of the database research and development work that has been carried out over a number of years at the Swidish National Central Bureau of Statistics. It describes the infological approach to databases that the author has introduced in 1973.

(Sundgren, 1978) B. Sundgren. Data Base Design in Theory and Practice, Towards an Integrated Methodology. Proc. 4th Int. Conf. on VLDB, West-Berlin, Germany, Sept 78, pp.3-16. (Also in Issues in DB Management. H. Weber and A.I. Wasserman (Eds), North-Holland, 1979, pp.3-23.)

The paper gives an overview of the database design process. Many problem areas are addressed in the paper, some of them are: purpose and role of a database, user participation, modelling of reality, information needs.

(Swartwout, 1977) D. Swartwout. An Access Path Specification Language for Restructuring Network Databases. Proc. ACM-SIGMOD Int. Conf. on Management of Data, Toronto, Canada, Aug 77, pp.88-101.

An approach to network database restructuring is presented in this paper; the approach is based on the Access Path Specification Language (APSL) which is a high-level non procedural language for specifying restructuring transformations of network databases. APSL is based on the Relational Interface Model of data, which permits a restricted network database to be viewed also as a relational database.

(Symons and Tijsma, 1982) C.R. Symons, P. Tijsma. A Systematic and Practical Approach to the Definition of Data. The Computer Jour., Vol.25, No.4, 1982, pp.410-422.

The data element analysis method described in this paper has been developed and used for five years at Philips. The method is based on data analysis and can be used to define data elements both in intercompany messages as well as in local systems and databases.

(Taggart and Tharp, 1977) W.M. Taggart, M.O. Tharp. A Survey of Information Requirements Analysis Techniques. Computing Surv., Vol.9, No.4, Dec 77, pp.273-290.

This survey covers a variety of approaches to the determination of information needs suggested during the previous decade.

(Taylor, 1980) R.W. Taylor. Using Generalized Data Translation Techniques for Database Interchange. IBM Res. Rep. RJ2866, IBM Res. Lab. San Jose, Jul 80, pp.13.

(Teorey and Fry, 1980) T.J. Teorey, J.P. Fry. The Logical Record Access Approach to Database Design. Computing Surv., Vol.12, No.2, Jun 80, pp.179-211.

This paper presents a practical stepwise database design methodology that derives a DBMS-processable database structure from a set of user information and processing requirements. Although the methodology emphasizes conceptual and implementation design, requirements analysis and physical design are also addressed. The methodology is illustrated with a detailed example. Performance trade-offs among multuple users of a single integrated database are considered, and the relationship between short-term design and design for flexibility to changing requirements is discussed.

(Teorey and Fry, 1982) T.J. Teorey, J.P. Fry. Design of Database Structures. Prentice-Hall, Englewood Cliffs, NJ, 1982, pp.xv+492.

The purpose of this book is to establish a consistent framework for multilevel database design; to define a workable methodology; and to describe a set of general principles, tools, and techniques for database design at each level.

(Tozer, 1976) E.E. Tozer. Database Systems Analysis and Design. Apr 76, pp.31.

This paper puts forward an overall view of system design which is intended to act as a constraining framework. It is based upon a pragmatic approach and is presented in a form which has been used on large scale implementation projects. This paper is extracted from a conference proceedings volume

but no useful information is included to complete the given
reference.

(Tsichritzis and Klug, 1978) D.   Tsichritzis, A.
Klug (Eds). The ANSI/X3/SPARC DBMS Framework Report
of the Study Group on Database Management Systems.
Inform. Syst., Vol.3, No.3, 1978, pp.173-191.

This report provides the generalised framework for the
description of database management systems developed by the
ANSI/X3/SPARC Study Group on DBMS.

(Tsichritzis and Lochovsky, 1982) D.C. Tsichritzis,
F.H.   Lochovsky.   Data Models.   Prentice-Hall,
Englewood Cliffs, NJ, 1982, pp.xiv+381.

Data models, as presented in this book, have been devised for
computer-oriented representation of information.   They are
powerful conceptual tools for the organisation and
representation of information. The book is divided into four
parts. The first part outlines the basic concepts used by all
data models; the second part describes the three most common
data models; the third part outlines four additional data
models which represent different approaches to data modelling.
And the fourth part deals with the use of data models for
database design and operation.

(Tsur and Zaniolo, 1984) S. Tsur, C. Zaniolo. An
Implementation of GEM - supporting a semantic data
model on a relational back-end.   In: Proc.
ACM-SIGMON Ann. Meeting.   B.   Yormark (Ed).
Boston, MA, Jun 84, pp.286-295.

The authors demonstrate the feasibility of extending a
relational DBMS into one supporting a semantic data model.
They present a system that consists of a UNIX-based front-end
that maps the GEM semantic data model and query language to an
underlying IDM 500 relational DB machine.

(Ullman, 1980) J.D. Ullman. Principles of Database
Systems. Computer Science Press, Potomac, MD, 1980,
pp.379.

In this book database ideas are explicitly related to
concepts from other areas of computing science, such as
programming languages, algorithms, and data structures.   The
book is mainly concentrated on the relational approach.

(Van Duyn, 1982) J. Van Duyn. Developing a Data Dictionary System. Prentice-Hall, Englewood Cliffs, NJ, 1982, pp.xiv+204.

The objective of this book is to provide a comprehensive, pragmatic source of knowledge about data dictionaries. Thus this book enhasizes its practical approach; sample applications of existing in-house developed and commercially available data dictionary are included in the text.

(Vetter and Maddison, 1981) M. Vetter, R.N. Maddison. Database Design Methodology. Prentice-Hall, Englewood Cliffs, NJ, 1981, pp.xii+306.

This book provides guidelines on how to define, structure, store and present data once the pertinent part of the information system has been identified.

(Wasserman and Botnick, 1981) A.I. Wasserman, K. Botnick. Annotated Bibliography on Data Design. SIGMOD RECORD, Vol.11, No.1, Jan 81, pp.46-77.

This is a selective bibliography of documents covering a wide range of topics on data structures and database design. The emphasis is given to those papers that attempt to develop a consistent approach to data design across the programming languages/database management interface and to those data design techniques that propose systematic methods for the design activity. The year span covered by the referred documents is 1969-80.

(Weber, 1976) H. Weber. A Semantic Model of Integrity Constraints on a Relational Data Base. In: (Nijssen, 1976a), pp.269-292.

The paper shows that the relational model does not provide all the necessary representational capabilities to allow a complete representation of the reality and a semantically correct sharing of the database among various user views. It introduces two types of integrity constraints to overcome this deficiencies.

(Weber and Wasserman, 1979) H. Weber, A.I. Wasserman (Eds). Issues in Data Base Management. North-Holland, Amsterdam, the Netherlands, 1979, pp.ix+263.

This volume contains material from the survey sessions held at
the 4th Int. Conf. on VLDB on Sept 13-15, 1978 in Berlin,
Germany.
Five subject areas were chosen for presentation and discussion
during   the   survey   sessions: DB Design;   DB Software
Engineering; DDB Systems; Impact of New Technologies;   and
DB Security and Privacy.
Each session encompassed a survey presentation and a panel
discussion.   The book contains a reprint of the survey
presentation and of the statements issued by the various panel
members.
The survey presentation of the DB Design session is (Sundgren,
1978), the panel discussion contains very useful comments.

(Weller and York, 1984) D.L. Weller, B.W. York. A
Relational   Representation   of an Abstract Type
System. IEEE Trans. on Software Engin., Vol.SE-10,
No.3, May 84, pp.303-309.

This paper proposes that databases have a type system
interface and describes a representation of a type system in
terms of relations.

(Whang et al, 1981) K.-Y. Whang, G. Wiederhold, D.
Sagalowicz.   Separability - An Approach to Physical
Database Design. Proc. 7th Int. Conf. on VLDB,
Cannes, France, Sept 81, pp.320-332.

A theoretical approach to the optimal design of a large
multiple physical database is presented.

(Whittington and Tully, 1982) R.P. Whittington,
C.J.   Tully.   A seven- subschema model for
evolutionary database development. Proc. of 2nd
British Nat. Conf. on DB, Bristol, England, Jul
82, pp.63-79.

The reported research is still in its early stages. It is too
soon to see the future of the presented ideas.

(Wiederhold, 1983) G. Wiederhold. Database Design
(2nd Ed). McGraw-Hill, New York, NY, 1983, pp.751.

This is the second improved edition of one of the most
important books in the database area; thus it is pertinent to
this bibliography as a useful general reading.

(Wilmot, 1984) R.B. Wilmot. Foreign Keys Decrease Adaptability of Database Designs. Comm. of the ACM, Vol.27, No.12, Dec 84, pp.1237-1243.

The author shows the limited adaptability of database designs incorporating foreign keys.

(Wilson, 1979) T.B. Wilson. Database Restructuring: Options and Obstacles. In: Proc. EURO IFIP 79. P.A. Samet (Ed), North-Holland, 1979, pp.567-573.

Database restructuring for CODASYL database systems is addressed in this paper. The commercial and experimental approaches to restructuring CODASYL-type databases available in 1979 are reviewed and the issues and problems discussed. The author attributes to the nature of the CODASYL approach the difficulty in developing effective restructuring methodologies for this type of DB systems.

(Wilson, 1980) T.B. Wilson. The Description and Usage of Evolving Schemas. Proc. COMPSAC 80, IEEE, Chicago, IL, Oct 80.

(Windsor, 1980) A.T. Windsor (Ed). Using the ICL Data Dictionary. Shiva Pub., Orpington, England, 1980, pp.153.

The ICL Data Dictionary System (DDS) has been the first commercial implementation of the British Computer Society DDS Working Party's proposal, see (BCS/DDSWP, 1977).
The aims of this book is twofold: i) to provide a consolidated reference for existing users, ii) to provide introductory material for new or potential DDS users and for those interested in the general use and potential of data dictionaries.

(Wong and Mylopoulos, 1977) H.K.T. Wong, J. Mylopoulos. Two Views of Data Semantics: A Survey of Data Models in Artificial Intellingence and Database Management. INFOR, Vol.15, No.3, Oct 77, pp.344-383.

The relationships between data models in database management and representations of knowledge in artificial intelligence are investigated in this paper.

(Wood-Harper   and   Fitzgerald,   1982)   A.T.
Wood-Harper, G. Fitzgerald. A Taxonomy of Current
Approaches to Systems Analysis. The Computer Jour.,
Vol.25, 1982, pp.12-16.

This paper classifies the six major approaches to systems
analysis in terms of the paradigms that they incorporate and
the conceptual models and objectives they hold.
The basic differences among these approaches are explained
together with reasons why these different approaches do exist.

(Yadav,   1983)   S.B.   Yadav.   Determing   an
Organization's Information Requirements: A State of
the Art Survey. DATA BASE, Vol.14, No.3, Spring 83,
pp.3-20.

This paper surveys the state of the art of methodologies for
information requirements determination of an organisation.

(Yao et al, 1982a) S.B.   Yao, S.B.   Navathe, J.L
Weldon,   T.L.   Kunii (Eds).   Data Base Design
Techniques I: Requirements and Logical Structures
Lecture   Notes   in   Computer   Science   No.132
Springer-Verlag, Berlin, Germany, 1982, pp.v+22
(Proc. of NYU Symp., New York, NY, May 78).
(Yao and Kunii, 1982) S.B. Yao, T.L. Kunii (Eds)
Data Base Design Techniques II: Physical Structure.
and Applications. Lecture Notes in Computer Science
No.133.   Springer-Verlag, Berlin, Germany, 1982
pp.v and 229-399 (Proc. Symp. on DB Engin., Tokio
Japan, Nov 79).

The New York University (NYU) Symposium on Data Base Design
(May 78) and the Symposium on Data Base Engineering (Nov 79)
were held to compare and summarise various newly developed
approaches to database design.
These two Lectures Notes volumes were compiled to further
disseminate the results presented to the conferences. These
volumes contain revised papers from the proceedings and
several new papers. They are a valuable reference for every
researcher of the field.

(Yao et al, 1982b) S.B. Yao, S.B.   Navathe, J.L
Weldon.   An Integrated Approach to Database Design
In: (Yao et al, 1982a), pp.1-30.

An integrated approach to research related to the problem o
database design is presented in this paper. A decompositio

of the database design process in five   phases   is   presented;
the   input,   processing   steps,   and output for each phase are
described.   Existing   approaches   to   database   design   are
reviewed and related to these five phases.

(Yao et al, 1982c) S.B.   Yao,   V.E.   Waddle,   B.C.
Housel.   View   Modeling   and   Integration Using the
Functional Data Model.   IEEE   Trans.   on   Software
Engin., Vol.SE-8, No.6, Nov 82, pp.544-553.

This paper reports on the development of a system for computer
aided   database   design (CADD).   The system is based on a data
model called   the   Functional   Data   Model   (FDM),   and   on   a
transaction   model   which   is   specified   via   the   Transaction
Specification Language (TASL).

(Yeh   and   Baker,   1977)   R.T.   Yeh,   J.W.   Baker.
Toward   a   Design   Methodology   for DBMS: a Software
Engineering Approach.   Proc.   3rd   Int.   Conf.   on
VLDB, Tokyo, Japan, Oct 77, pp.16-27.

The methodology presented in   this   paper   consists   of   three
interacting   models: a   model   for   the   system structure, a
hierarchical performance evaluation model,   and   a   model   for
design   structure   documentation,   which   are   developed
concurrently through a top-down design process.

(Yormark, 1977) B.   Yormark.   The   ANSI/X3/SPARC/SG
DBMS Architecture.   In: (Jardine, 1977), pp.1-21.

This paper presents the architecture for DBMS developed by the
ANSI/X3/SPARC   Study Group on Data Base Management Systems, as
it was presented in the interim report of the group.
This architecture is the so-called three   levels   approach   to
data   base modelling that consists of the conceptual, external
and internal levels.   The concepts   of   conceptual   level   and
conceptual schema are introduced for the first time.

(Zaniolo, 1979) C.   Zaniolo.   Multimodel   external
schemas   for   CODASYL   data base management systems.
In: Database Architecture,   G.   Bracchi   and   G.M.
Nijssen (Eds), North-Holland, 1979, pp.171-190.

The   problem   of   designing   and   supporting   relational   and
hierarchical views over CODASYL network schemas is considered.

(Zaniolo and Melkanoff, 1982) C. Zaniolo, M.A. Melkanoff. A Formal Approach to the Definition and the Design of Conceptual Schemata for Database Systems. ACM Trans. on DB Syst., Vol.7, No.1, Mar 82, pp.24-59.

A formal approach is described in this paper for the definition and the design of conceptual database diagrams which are useful in designing various forms schemas and in the role of conceptual schemas for a three levels DBMS architecture.

(Zimmermann, 1980) H. Zimmermann. OSI Reference Model - The ISO Model of Architecture for Open Systems Interconnection. IEEE Trans. on Comm., Vol.COM-28, No.4, Apr 80, pp.425-432.

The ISO/TC97/SC16 subcommittee for "Open Systems Interconnection" (OSI) was created in 1977. The first priority of this subcommittee was to develop an architecture for OSI which could serve as a framework for the definition of standard protocols. This paper introduces the ISO/OSI model which is introduced in full in (OSI, 1981) and (OSI, 1982). See also (desJardins, 1981), (Mohan and Popescu-Zeletin, 1982), (Popescu-Zeletin and Weber, 1980) and (Steel, 1982).

4291